MENSA

MIGHTY MIND BENDERS

RIDDLES & CONUNDRUMS

THIS IS A CARLTON BOOK

This edition published by Limited Editions

First published in 1995 by Stanley Paul & Co. Ltd

An imprint of Random House UK Limited
20 Vauxhall Bridge Road, London SW1 2SA

Text and puzzles © Mensa Limited 1995
Design and artwork copyright © Carlton Books Limited 1995

A CIP catalogue record for this book
is available from the British Library

ISBN 0-09-180491-4

Designed by Jacqui Sheard

Printed in Italy

MENSA

MIGHTY MIND BENDERS

RIDDLES & CONUNDRUMS

Robert Allen

LIMITED EDITIONS
BOOKTITLES

INTRODUCTION

IN THE TIME IT TAKES YOU to crack a handful of the Supersleuth lateral thinking puzzles contained within this book, you could have mown the lawn, washed the car or decorated the spare room. The fiendishly cunning Mind Maze in the middle of the book will occupy hours which you could have devoted to higher and nobler causes, or you could have popped out for a few drinks. But there is nothing more enjoyable or more satisfying than solving puzzles, and here are puzzles of every kind in abundance.

If you like puzzles you will like Mensa. It is the only society I know of that you get to join just by being good at puzzling. We have 120,000 members throughout the world so, wherever you live, there is probably a branch near you. But if you have any trouble finding your local branch, write to us at British Mensa, Mensa House, St. John's Square, Wolverhampton WV2 4AH, England.

I would like to thank Tim Sell for his excellent illustrations and Josephine Fulton for the devious products of her fertile brain.

ROBERT ALLEN
Editorial Director, Mensa Publications
October, 1994

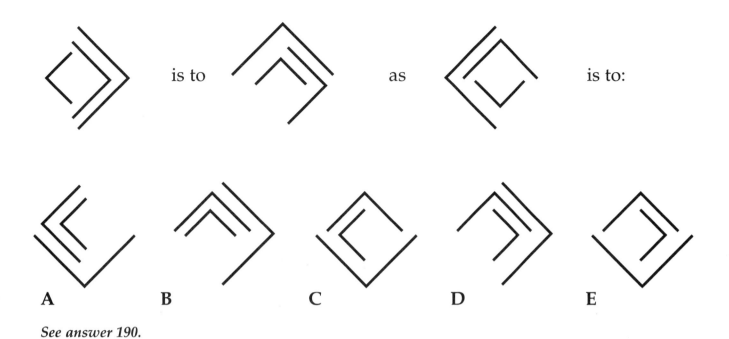

is to   as   is to:

A   B   C   D   E

See answer 190.

Which is the odd one out?

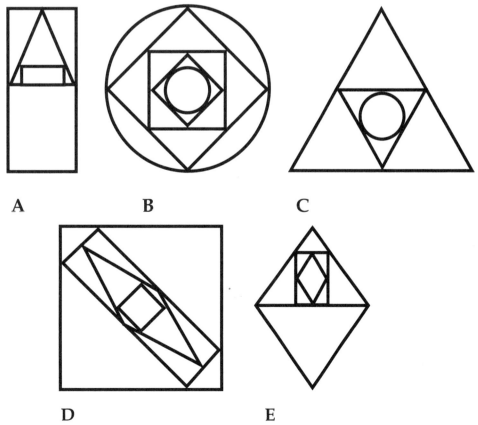

A   B   C

See answer 42.   D   E

'I know a question which can never be answered "Yes",' said Sam. 'So do I,' said Joe. 'How about "Are you a gorilla?", I could never answer that with a yes.' 'Oh, yes you could,' objected Sam. 'You would just have to lie. The question I have in mind could never be answered with a yes even by the most brazen liar.' What was the question Sam had in mind?

See answer 64.

Which of the following forms a perfect triangle when combined with the picture on the right?

A

B

C

D

E

See answer 191.

1 Insert the correct mathematical signs to make the following calculations work:

7 8 20 32 = 44

9 3 42 12 = 94.5

8 2 12 9 = 37

6 7 15 13 = 44

5 32 6 20 = 18.75

See answer 151.

2 Look at the clock faces shown below. Choose one to continue the series.

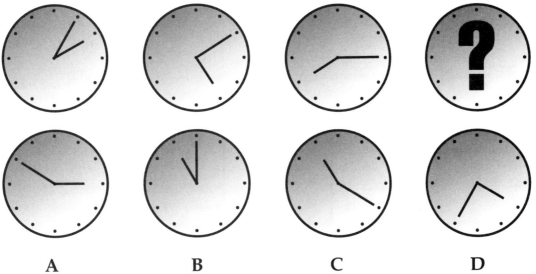

A   B   C   D

See answer 48.

Which is the odd one out?

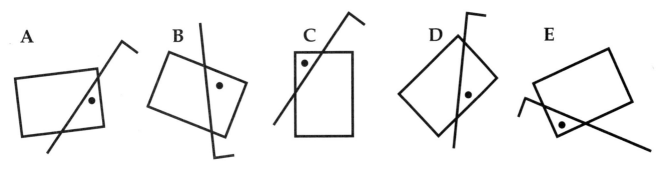

See answer 181.

1 A frog sits on a lily pad in the precise middle of a circular pond with a radius of 6 metres (19 feet). He jumps straight towards the edge of the pond a distance of 3 metres (9 ft, 6 ins) but this tires him and every subsequent jumps is precisely half the distance of the jump before (ie, 1.5 metres (4 ft 9 ins), 75cm (2 ft, 4 ins), etc). How many jumps does it take him to reach the edge of the pond?

See answer 6.

2 How many grooves were there on an old-fashioned vinyl record?

See answer 49.

3 Which is correct, 'All fish have warm blood' or 'All fishes are warm-blooded'?

See answer 54.

4 Alex and Georgina were born at the same hour of the same day to the same mother in the same hospital. They have the same father and yet they are not twins. Why ?

See answer 118.

By taking away four matches from this diagram leave eight small squares.

See answer 144.

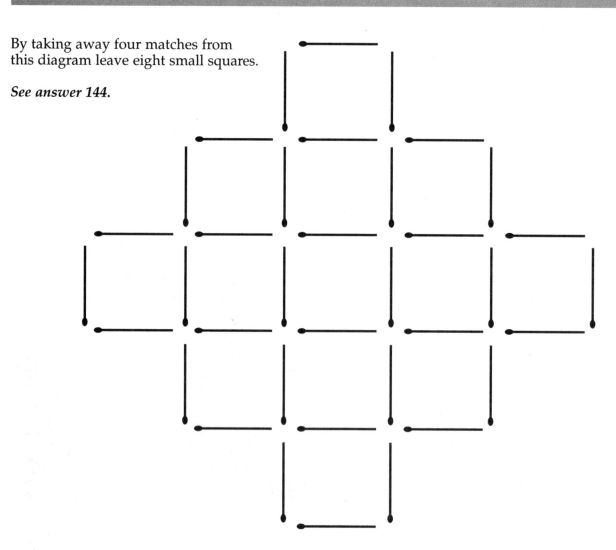

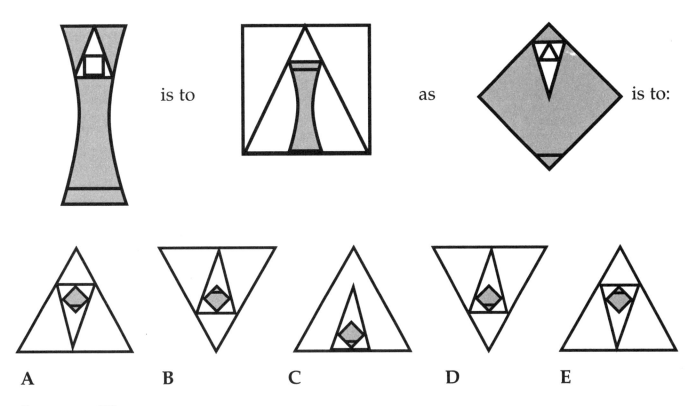

See answer 192.

The British used to use gold sovereigns. The 1883 sovereign contained exactly the same amount of gold as the 1884 one. Even so, 1884 sovereigns are worth more than 1883 sovereigns. Why? There is no special historical significance to the date 1883.

See answer 63.

Which is the odd one out?

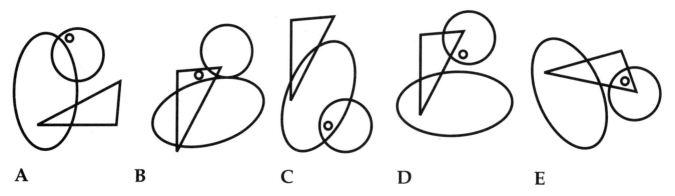

A   B   C   D   E

See answer 193.

After a VIP party, the floor was littered with the torn up name tags of the rich and famous. Try to put them back together to discover the guest list. All the guests were actors.

MO RO THAU MAT ORE WAL
MAR ROB JO MAN LEW
TER LON LEN ALE DAY SKI
FORD BRAN IEL RED CY
CAR AL IS DIA DY
AN BILL ERT SHEP TER
FOS DIN HERD DUD DO
CLAU DAN WOO DIE LEY POL

See answer 168.

12

1 Before Sir Richard Burton attempted to discover the source of the Nile what was the world's longest river?

See answer 1.

2 Though the discoverers of Antarctica (South Pole) were often close to starvation they would never touch the meat of the Polar Bear even though they possessed the means to kill one. Why?

See answer 17.

3 The shamans of Central Asia knew of an ancient and ingenious means of passing right through solid walls. What was it?

See answer 30.

4 In the early 18th century Mrs Abigail Eischrank of Cambridge, Massachusetts, gave birth to 13 children. Exactly half of them were girls. Explain.

See answer 46.

5 Leonardo da Vinci carried out the following experiment. He held a sphere of very thin fragile glass above a floor of solid stone. When he dropped it the sphere fell two metres (6 feet, 6 inches) without breaking. How?

See answer 5.

Another series of clock faces. Again it is up to you to work out the logic behind the series and pick a clock to replace the question mark.

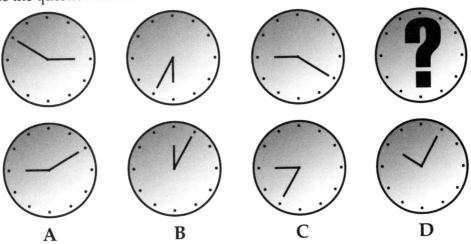

A   B   C   D

See answer 153.

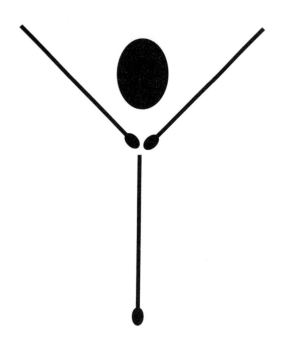

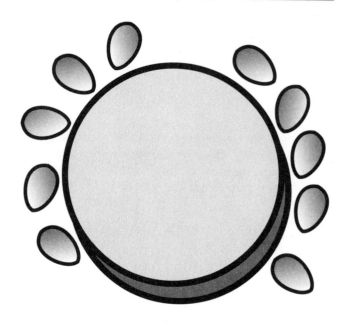

1 The diagram above is made up of matchsticks and represents a dry martini with an olive in the glass. Move one matchstick to place the olive outside the glass.

See answer 60.

2 This is a very old American puzzle but it has lost none of its tantalizing qualities with the passage of time. The diagram represents a round tablecloth. You have a supply of eggs and are invited to place one on the cloth. Your opponent then takes a turn. No eggs must be touching and you are not allowed to move an egg once it has been placed. The winner is the person who places the last egg. There is a way to win every time. What is it?

See answer 7.

QUICK WIT

*I*n 1993, 78-year-old Sergeant Noboru Yamamoto was discovered living on a remote Pacific island firmly under the impression that World War II was still on. He was eventually persuaded to return to Japan, where he was immediately surrounded by his remaining relatives and hordes of journalists. Suddenly a young man pushed to the front of the crowd, shot Yamamoto several times, and then swiftly left the room. No one took the slightest notice. Why? The young man did not know the sergeant and his motive was not any form of revenge.

See answer 9.

1 What has 21 spots but is never ill?

See answer 80.

2 What was the first man-made object to travel faster than the speed of sound?

See answer 62.

BRAIN TWISTERS   Puzzle 18

Which is the odd one out?

b   T   W   O   U

A   B   C   D   E

See answer 22.

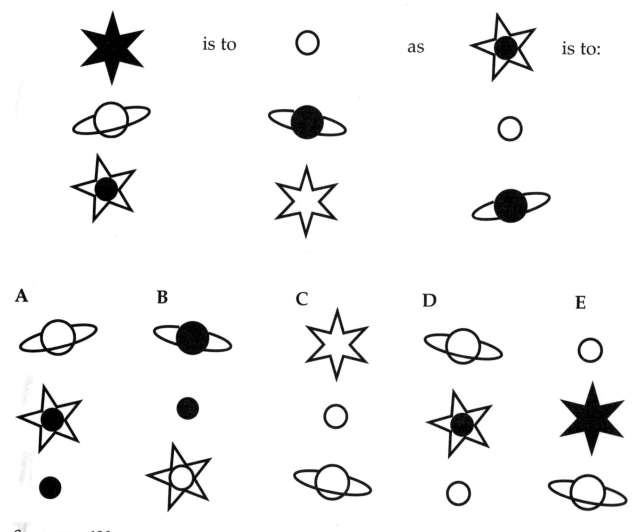

See answer 196.

Which is the odd one out?

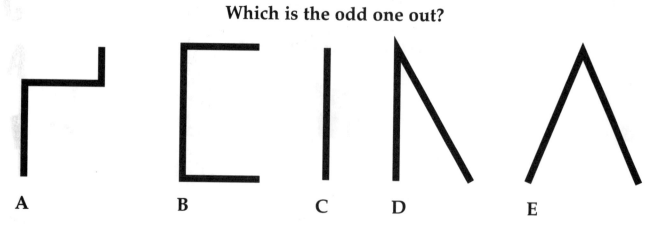

See answer 213.

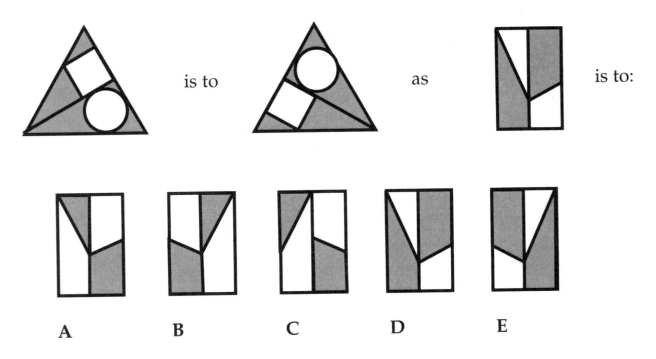

is to ... as ... is to:

A   B   C   D   E

See answer 182.

Someone has made a mistake decorating this cake. Can you correct the pattern?

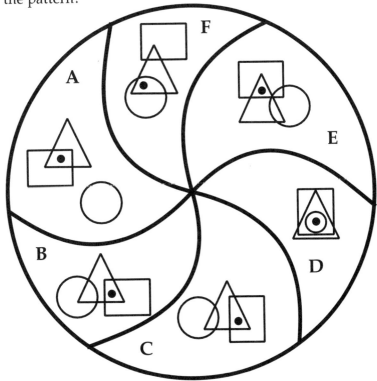

See answer 156.

1 Dave went with his uncle to the movies. They went up to the ticket kiosk and Dave had to pay, as usual. But that was not the worst of it. The ticket lady said, 'You can go in but not your friend.' Why wouldn't she let Dave's uncle in? He was smartly dressed and had often been to that cinema before without any trouble.

See answer 31.

2 In a run-down saloon in a small town west of the Pecos, One-Eyed Pete and his gang sat playing poker. There were five men round the table. A rougher, tougher looking bunch you never saw in your life. Just to be allowed to join the gang you had to skin your own grandma with a rusty potato peeler. After several games one of the men eyed the dealer narrowly and drawled, 'I says you're cheatin'!' It was an unwise comment. The dealer whipped out a gun and shot the offender dead. Naturally someone sent for the sheriff. He was a giant of a man who never went anywhere without two Colt .45s hanging from his belt. He was so mean and tough that he had skinned both his grandmas in a manner too horrible to relate. However, even though he was a stranger to fear, and the incident had been witnessed by everyone in the bar, he was unable to arrest any of the men who had taken part in the game. Why?

See answer 82.

Which of the following comes next in the sequence? *See answer 184.*

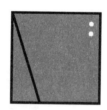
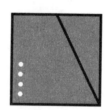
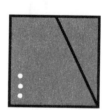

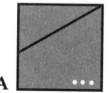 A
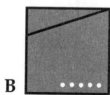 B
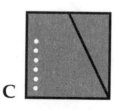 C
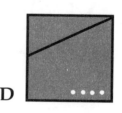 D
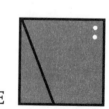 E

QUICK WIT

In the pioneer days of America a man lived on his ranch a few miles out of town. One night his wife was taken sick and he had to ride into town to get a doctor. He owned three horses but one was itself sick, another was too old to make the trip and there was no way he was ever going to ride the third. Why not?

He had only just bought the third horse and there was nothing wrong with it or with himself. In the stable there was no shortage of saddles and tack. What was the problem?

See answer 26.

HEADSCRATCHERS

The circles of letters below contain the names of three works of literature (one French, one from the Middle East, one American). Can you unravel them?

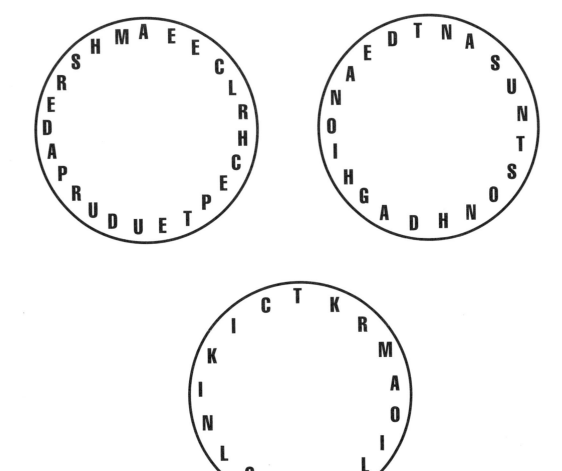

See answer 160.

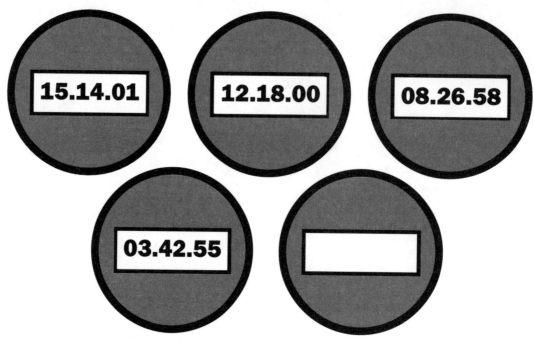

Have a look at these strange watches. By cracking the logic which connects them you should be able to work out what time should be shown on the face of the fifth watch.

See answer 66.

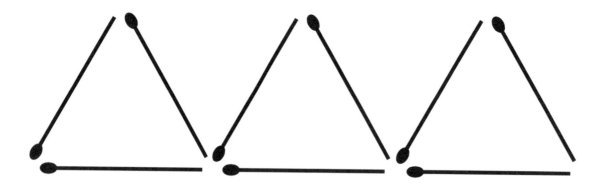

Take 9 matches and lay them out in three triangles. By moving three matches try to make five triangles.

See answer 141.

If you look at the grid carefully you will be able to find the names of three international airports cunningly concealed. The names wind through the grid like a snake so, once you have discovered one of them, it should be possible to discover the others.

See answer 157.

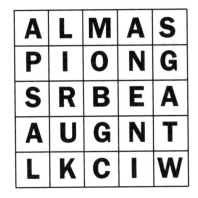

1 Sue Sugar had toothache. She went to the only dentists in town where she was greeted by Dr Molar and Dr Bicuspid, the partners. She noticed that whereas Dr Molar had a wonderful mouthful of teeth, his partner's teeth seemed in urgent need of attention. With which partner should she book her appointment?

See answer 33.

2 Six men drove over 240 km (150 miles) in a car at an average speed of 100 k/h (62.5 mph). The trip took 2.4 hours. When they unpacked their luggage they realised that the car had a flat during the whole journey. Why had they not noticed this before?

See answer 27.

Which of the following forms a perfect circle when combined with the diagram on the right?

See answer 183.

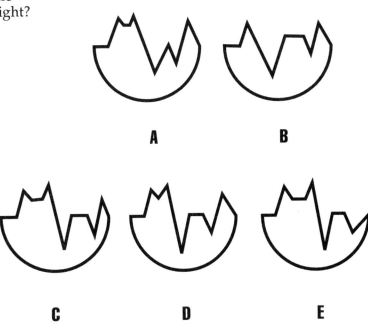

A   B

C   D   E

1 A train crossing from France to Germany suffered a terrible accident exactly on the border. According to international law in which country should the survivors be buried?

See answer 198.

2 Are there earthquakes on the Moon?

See answer 23.

Use 16 matches to make this figure. Now add eight more matches to divide the shape into four equal pieces.

See answer 149.

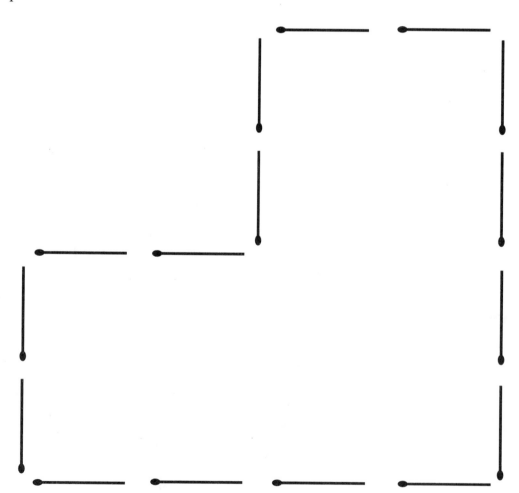

What comes next in the sequence?

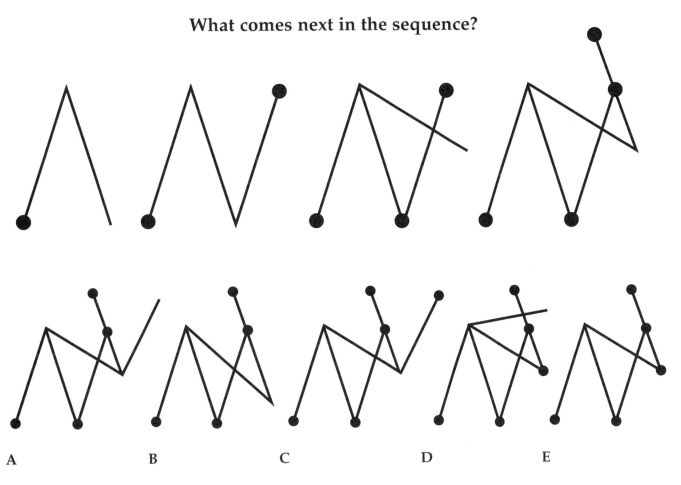

A   B   C   D   E

See answer 194.

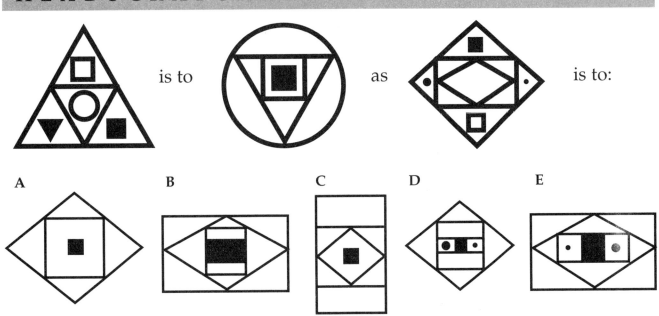

is to   as   is to:

A   B   C   D   E

See answer 215.

Which cube can be made using:

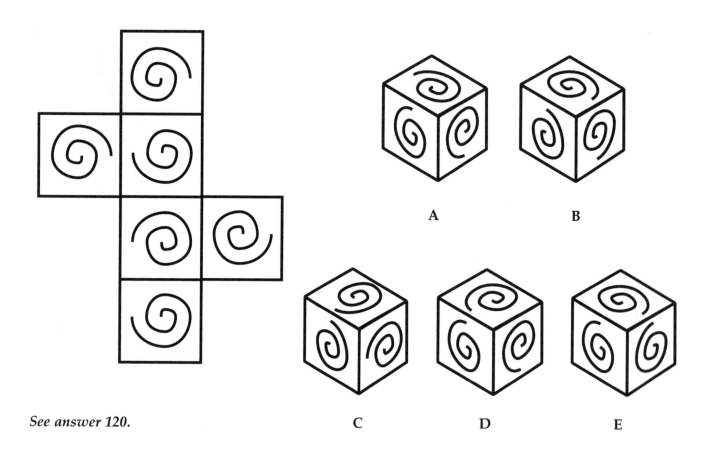

See answer 120.

Which is the odd one out?

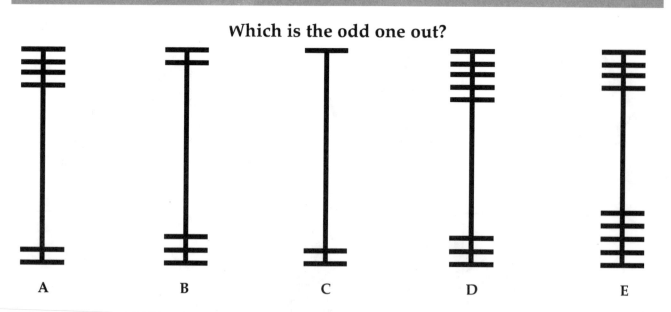

See answer 78.

Ali ben-Ibrahim was a salt dealer in old Baghdad. Every day he went from his home just outside the city to the market with two huge sacks of salt tied to the back of his donkey. His donkey was a small, evil-smelling brute called Roxanna. It was, however, not lacking in the brains department. One hot day, as they passed along the banks of the Tigris, it broke free from Ali and plunged into the cool water. When the irate salt-seller finally persuaded the beast to leave the river it immediately noticed that much of the salt had dissolved and its load was therefore considerably lighter. After that, no matter how hard Ali tried, he could not prevent the donkey from diving into the river and ruining its load of salt. But when it came to lateral thinking Ali himself was no slouch. One day he loaded up the donkey as usual and, as usual, the animal plunged into the river. Then it learned its lesson and never tried that trick again. What had Ali done?

See answer 34.

1 When the police arrived the man was lying under the car dead. Investigations revealed that although he was not the car's owner he was the last person to drive it. The car had last been driven that morning but the man's time of death was established at about 3pm. The car's owner was discovered in the south of France. No one else was involved in the affair and eventually the police and the coroner were satisfied that no crime had been committed. What is the explanation?

See answer 28.

2 Andy's aunt had lived all her adult life in Los Angeles having moved there when she married an American. She had lost touch with Andy's mother, her sister, for over 25 years. Then she suddenly wrote to say she was coming back for a holiday. Andy's mother gave him the flight number and asked him to pick his aunt up from Heathrow Airport. 'But how will I recognize her, I've never even seen a photograph!' he objected. 'And she's never seen a photograph of you,' added his mother cheerfully. 'But don't worry you won't miss her.' And he didn't, but how?

See answer 195.

What comes next in the sequence?

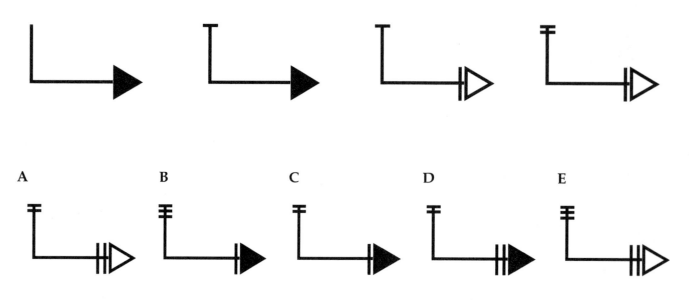

A   B   C   D   E

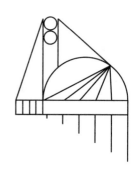

See answer 119.

Which of the following will be shaped like the diagram below if a single line of any shape but not overlapping any existing line, is added?

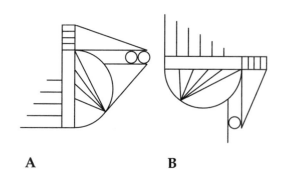

A   B

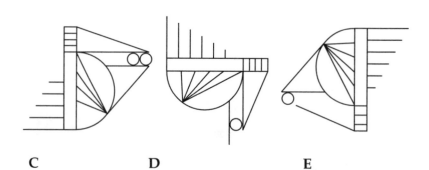

C   D   E

See answer 200.

Professor Potts has had a disaster. A shelf in his museum gave way and ten priceless busts of Roman emperors have been smashed. Fortunately, each had a name plate on it. Can you put the fractured names back together?

AU PA TI VALE
NE TIAN
DIO AU GAL CA BER DI
TUS LA US TRA GUS SIAN
RO BA VES CL CLE
IUS RIAN LI GU JAN

See answer 170.

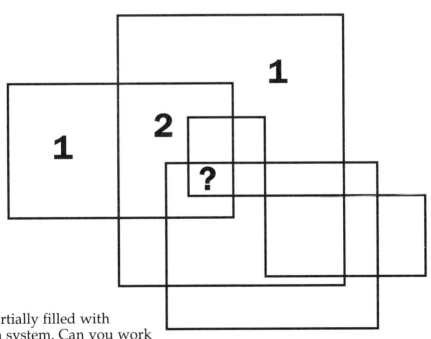

This figure has been partially filled with numbers according to a system. Can you work out the logic of the system and replace the question mark with a number?

See answer 68.

Try to work out the fiendish logic behind this series of clocks and replace the question mark.

See answer 154.

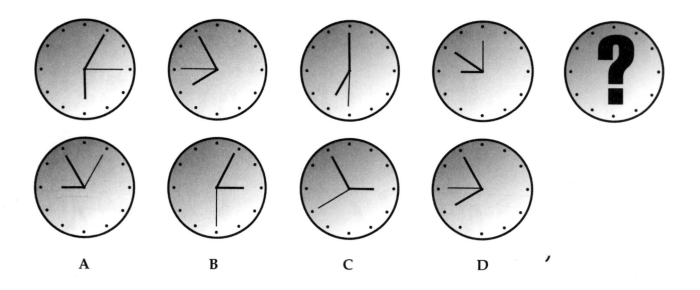

A   B   C   D

Which is the odd one out?

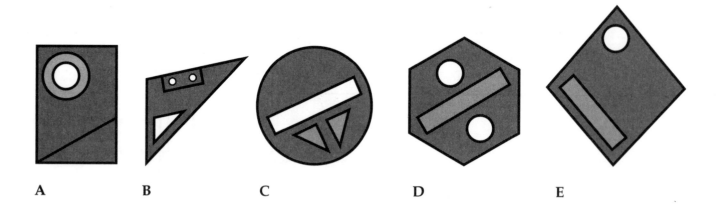

A   B   C   D   E

See answer 185.

1 After a long and arduous journey your ship reaches the sea which is your destination. However, there is no water to be seen anywhere. In fact there never was any water and you knew that perfectly well before you set out. So why did you navigate your ship to this sea?

See answer 163.

2 Sid Lightly always moans that if only people told the truth he would sell more of his goods. What does he make?

See answer 18.

3 Thomas and Craig go collecting sea shells. They take bag with them to hold their booty. Without knowing its dimensions can you work out how many sea shells they can put in the empty bag?

See answer 199.

4 Albert Coley is a fishmonger. He stands 6ft 6ins (2 metres) in his socks, takes size XXL in clothes and wears size 14 (50) shoes. What do you think he weighs?

See answer 127.

5 Sam Somnolent wanted a good night's rest. He went to bed at 8.30pm, wound up his 30-year-old alarm clock and set it to wake him at 9am. How many hours' sleep did Sam get?

See answer 211.

6 A man and his wife were driving rapidly through town late at night. Suddenly the car broke down. The man had to get help but was nervous about leaving his wife alone at that hour. However, there was absolutely no question of her coming too. Eventually he told her to lock all the doors, keep the windows shut and wait for him to return. Under no circumstances whatsoever was she to let anyone else into the car. The wife did as she was told, but, even so, when the man returned to the locked car his wife was entertaining two strangers. What had happened?

See answer 15.

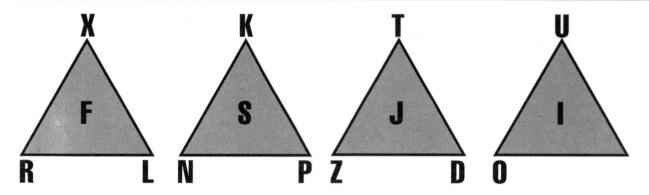

Look at these triangles. Can you work out what the missing letter is? *See answer 88.*

SUPER SLEUTH   Puzzle 48

1 How many times can you divide 345.6754 by 23.854?

See answer 36.

2 Ben Bright was a smart kid. He bet all the other kids in his class that they couldn't stick a pin in a fully inflated balloon without bursting it. He was right, they couldn't. Each loser had to give him their lunch money and by the end of the day he was quite rich. The other kids insisted that the trick was impossible but Ben did it easily. How?

See answer 19.

3 Young Ben Bright had another good idea. He bet his friends that they couldn't take hold of the ends of a piece of string and, without letting go, tie a knot in the middle of the string. After they had all failed miserably he showed them how it was done. What did he do?

See answer 164.

QUICK WIT   Puzzle 49

Khalil ben-Omar became Calif of Baghdad. Shortly after taking up his new position one of his advisors pointed out to him a little scruffy fellow riding a donkey in through the city gates. 'That man,' said the advisor, 'is a trader from Pakistan. His name is Zulfiqa Khan and he is the biggest rogue in the entire country. Don't let his appearance fool you. He's hugely rich and for years he has been making a fortune out of smuggling but we've never been able to catch him at it.' The Calif was intrigued and ordered that the smuggler should be searched rigorously every he time he entered or left the city. So each day Zulfiqa came riding into the city on his donkey and each day he was searched. Each evening he left on his donkey and each evening he was searched. Nothing was found. But all the time he grew richer and richer. At last the Calif could stand it no longer and he had Zulfiqa summoned to him. 'All right,' he said. 'I admit defeat'. You have been smuggling for years and I have never caught you. Just tell me how you did it and I will let you marry my daughter and make you one of the richest men in Baghdad.' What was Zulfiqa Khan smuggling?

See answer 116.

1 Sergeant Smashem of the Traffic Division reported an accident. A truck and twelve cars had been crushed when a bridge collapsed on them. The truck was badly damaged but the driver escaped from the cab without injury. When the sergeant arrived on the scene, there was no sign of any car drivers. Why not? There was no suggestion that any car driver was in any way to blame for the accident.

See answer 39.

2 One month of the year, February, has 28 or 29 days. How many months have 30 days?

See answer 10.

3 Sam Midas the Director of Midas Inc phones his wife to say he'll be home for dinner. 'Hi, honey, I'm just leaving the office now and I'll be home in ten minutes.' 'OK, darling,' says his wife, 'I'll see you soon.' Sam lives very near his office so he leaves at 6.30 and arrives home at 6.43. Just as he is getting out of the car his wife rushes from the house, boxes his ears and shouts, 'If you ever do that again I'll divorce you!' What did Sam do?

See answer 206.

4 A woman dropped a few coins in a beggar's bowl. The woman is the beggar's sister but the beggar is not the woman's brother. How are they related?

See answer 197.

All these famous playrights have had the vowels removed from their names and the first name joined to the surname. Can you sort them out? (The nationalities are given in brackets to help you.)

1. DWRDLB (American)
2. SMLBCKTT (Irish)
3. BRTHLTBRCHT (German)
4. NLCWRD (English)
5. NTNCHKV (Russian)
6. RTHRMLLR (American)
7. LGPRNDLL (Italian)
8. JNRCN (French)
9. SPHCLS (Greek – one word)
10. TNNSSWLLMS (American)

See answer 161.

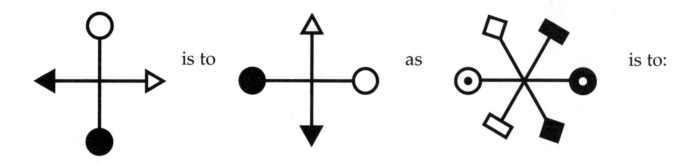

is to

as

is to:

A B C D E

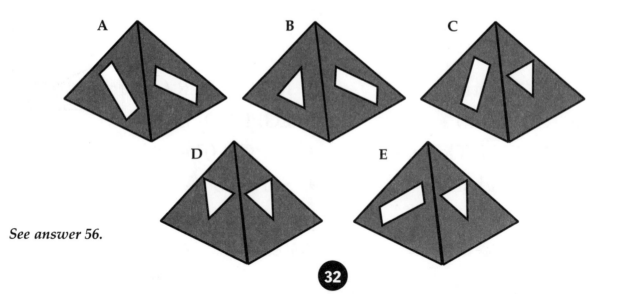

See answer 201.

Which of the following can be
constructed using:

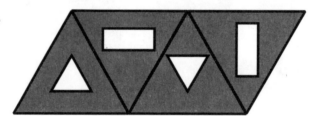

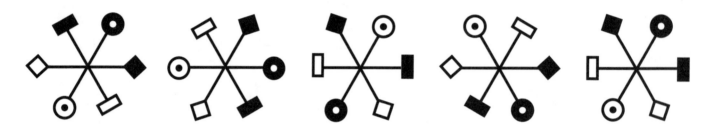

A B C

D E

See answer 56.

1 If a man lives in Seattle why can't he be buried in Birmingham?

See answer 2.

2 Do the British have a Fourth of July?

See answer 203.

3 Dave and his brother Bob married Sue and Hannah who are both sisters. However Dave and Bob have different in-laws. How can this be?

See answer 45.

Hidden in this grid are 11 international airports. The names follow each other and meander in a snake-like route through the grid. When you discover the first name you should be able to find the other 10.

See answer 158.

D	A	L	A	M	A	N	D	A	R
E	H	M	A	A	L	A	S	S	E
R	O	N	E	B	I	T	T	E	N
A	C	A	R	K	Z	E	R	A	U
H	H	E	B	E	N	I	T	O	J
O	I	L	L	U	A	G	E	D	S
Y	M	S	O	C	H	A	R	L	E
O	I	A	P	L	E	N	O	T	S
C	N	H	C	I	T	Y	H	O	U
C	M	W	O	R	H	T	A	E	H

Which of the following comes next in the sequence?

Y	V	S	P
H	J	M	Q
P	H	D	B

A	B	C	D	E
M	Q	N	M	Q
V	U	T	V	V
B	A	B	A	B

See answer 202.

Which is the odd one out?

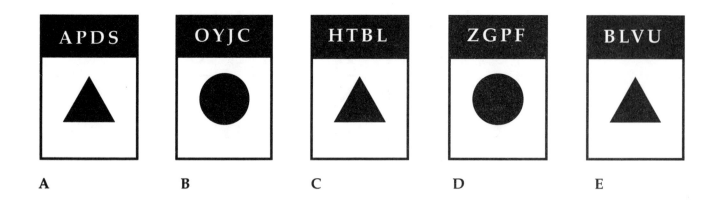

| APDS | OYJC | HTBL | ZGPF | BLVU |
| A | B | C | D | E |

See answer 44.

Which is the odd one out?

See answer 188.

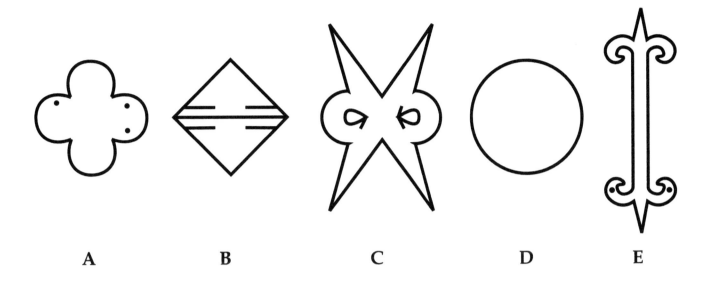

A friend of mine used to bet unwary tourists a pint of beer that they couldn't take six matches and lay them out in such a way that each touched the other five. He was never known to pay for his own beer!

See answer 150.

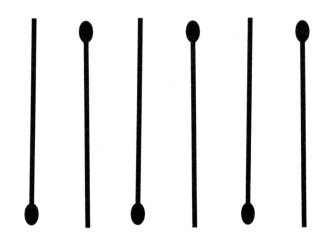

Take a postcard and a pair of scissors. Now cut the postcard in such a way that you can step right through the hole in the middle. Impossible? No, with a little ingenuity you should be able to create a hole through which your entire body can pass.

See answer 77.

1 Jim White watched in exasperation as the soccer team he had led to world fame over five years was trounced by Brazil. It was just awful! No matter how much he bellowed advice and encouragement nobody took the slightest notice. He almost wept with sheer frustration. At last the whole dismal affair was over and Brazil won by such a huge margin that it went into the record books. Yet, oddly, when the next day's newspapers came out, Jim, far from being attacked, was extravagantly praised. Why?

See answer 51.

2 A man went to the garage to have an electrical fault on his car repaired. Unfortunately the mechanic was ill and therefore the work could not be done. Determined not to waste his trip the man decided to put his car through the car wash. He closed the sun roof, retracted the radio aerial, drove the car into the tunnel and then got out and waited outside for the washing to begin. It was only when he had pushed the button and the washing cycle had started that the man began to bellow with rage. Why?

See answer 16.

QUICK WIT

The Wigan Philharmonia Orchestra was touring America for the first time and things were not going well. Their performances had been widely criticized and, in particular Albert Winterbottom, the conductor, had come in for some sharp criticism. One evening after a particularly awful peformance a man in the audience stood up and yelled, 'Winterbottom, you shouldn't be allowed out, after what you did to that score you should be a butcher instead of a musician!' Albert, unable to stand any more criticism, pulled a gun and shot the man dead in front of the entire audience. The trial was a foregone conclusion and, before long Albert Winterbottom faced the electric chair. However, no matter how many times they tried to execute him nothing happened. The equipment was dismantled, checked, put together again and still didn't work. Why?

See answer 81.

SUPER SLEUTH

1 Police Officer Gribble was on patrol when he noticed a small girl turn the corner and pass him going down the street. He smiled as she passed but took no further notice. After a few minutes walk the girl came round the corner again and, once more she passed him. This had happened three more times and each time the girl seemed more agitated. At last he could stand it no longer. 'Why are you walking round and round the block,' he demanded. What was the reply?

See answer 53.

2 Emily was delighted when she found that frogs had settled in the garden pond. Sometimes there was a big green one, sometimes a brown, and she saw a couple of little ones too. Then she got to wondering just how many frogs actually lived in the pond. She tried to count them but could never reach the same total twice. Once she was quite sure there were six when, without warning, a completely new frog appeared. Without draining the pond what would be the best way of finding how many frogs there are?

See answer 4.

The pictures illustrate different views of one cube. What does the side indicated by the X look like?

A   B   C   D   E

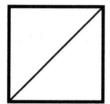  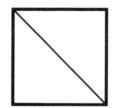 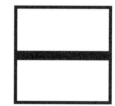 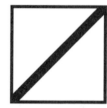

See answer 13.

Which of the following patterns will match the conditions of the diagram below if a single straight line is added?

See answer 205.

1 In Dead Men's Gulch, Colorado, there was a barber who had a hold over the local mayor. The mayor was manipulated into passing a law that no man might shave himself and no man might grow a beard. This was all very well and the barber did well out of it but, nevertheless, even one so rich was not above the law. Who shaved the barber?

See answer 65.

2 Victor Serebriakoff, International President of Mensa, once made up a poem about hyperbolic acid, a substance so corrosive that it would eat its way through anything. One day Sir Clive Sinclair, the inventor and British Mensa Chairman, phoned his old friend with some stunning news: 'Victor, you'll never believe this but I have actually invented your hyperbolic acid! Stay where you are and I'll dash round to your house with a flask of it right now.' Victor replaced the phone and chuckled to himself. How could he tell he was being teased?

See answer 11.

Which of the following comes next in the sequence?

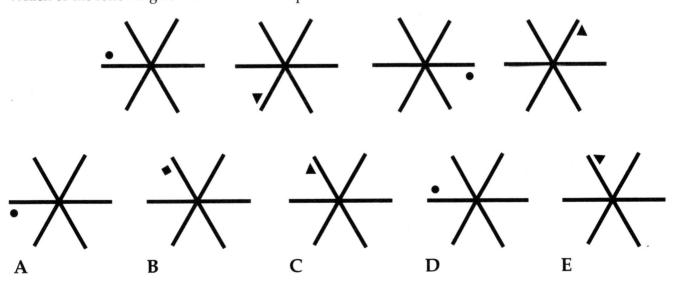

See answer 187.

You are lost in Paris, but if you search carefully you will find the following well-known places cunningly concealed. Names may be spelt in any direction, not necessarily in a straight line.

RUE DE RIVOLI   BOIS DE BOULOGNE
MOULIN ROUGE   CHAMPS ELYSEES
CLICHY   RUE LAFAYETTE
PERE LACHAISE   SACRE COEUR
ARC DE TRIOMPHE

MADELEINE   MONTMARTRE
OPERA   GARE DE LYON
LOUVRE   JARDIN DES PLANTES

See answer 165.

M	I	F	T	E	P	Z	L	E	I	R	U	E	P	D	T	M	E	R	B
A	A	D	I	H	U	Z	N	E	S	H	A	L	E	R	O	H	N	E	O
N	G	D	H	T	E	I	E	M	S	A	A	A	E	R	M	S	U	E	M	I
C	H	H	E	S	E	Y	O	E	S	F	G	S	E	U	T	B	L	U	S
A	R	D	E	L	L	I	W	N	A	F	A	O	L	E	I	I	L	T	D
G	A	R	D	E	O	N	D	E	I	Y	Y	N	A	W	N	L	L	R	E
Y	T	R	E	O	A	M	T	H	M	R	E	I	C	L	H	R	A	S	B
O	D	E	C	H	D	E	P	E	O	W	T	L	H	T	E	Y	O	S	O
U	T	H	C	T	Y	A	R	S	P	S	T	E	A	F	R	A	N	U	U
M	E	A	T	H	E	C	O	M	E	O	Z	E	D	I	O	D	E	G	L
M	J	A	R	D	I	N	D	O	U	L	E	G	S	S	A	C	R	E	O
C	H	C	T	P	R	E	E	R	N	H	Y	R	E	R	U	E	O	C	G
A	R	A	E	R	S	A	S	A	D	T	I	S	D	J	U	I	K	H	N
T	C	A	R	S	A	D	P	F	N	I	S	E	I	S	T	L	E	T	E
C	T	O	H	C	I	S	L	E	L	I	B	E	R	T	E	L	I	L	E
L	E	P	R	E	D	D	A	N	T	E	S	S	E	A	Y	L	T	T	S
I	Y	E	S	T	E	G	M	T	M	O	N	T	M	A	R	T	R	E	O
C	T	R	E	T	Y	R	U	E	D	E	R	I	V	O	L	I	D	O	N
H	H	A	R	W	A	T	H	E	Y	A	B	E	E	N	E	T	U	O	R
Y	N	D	I	O	M	P	H	E	H	V	E	L	O	U	V	R	E	E	A

Captain Franklin and his crew were lost in the icy sea off Greenland. Food was low and, what was worse, they had run out of water. 'If we drink the sea water we'll die,' said the First Mate. 'No need for that, Mr MacTavish,' replied Franklin, 'the sea water round here is quite drinkable.' What did he mean?

See answer 50.

HEADSCRATCHERS

1 Look in a mirror. You left hand seems to have become your right and your right is now apparently your left. You have been laterally reversed! Why does the mirror not reverse you vertically as well?

See answer 117.

2 What has three hands, the second hand really being the third?

See answer 3.

3 Two men are charged with murder. One committed the act but the other is quite innocent. The judge is in a quandry as to how to punish the guilty whilst letting the innocent man go free. Finally he calls for an eminent doctor to advise him. Why?

See answer 84.

4 Smart Alec sat in biology class with a smug grin on his face. 'What are you looking so pleased about?' asked the teacher with a feeling of impending doom. 'I know something that has four legs and two arms,' announced Alec proudly. The teacher racked his brains but could think of no creature which fitted the description. What did Alec mean?

See answer 71.

5 'You're really going to fly around the Earth from North to South?' said the young man to the aviator. 'I'll bet you'll need your thermal underwear when you pass over the Poles!' 'Actually,' the intrepid flyer replied, 'the Poles are the least of my worries I shall have to pass twice over a much colder area than that.' What could it be?

See answer 125.

1 What is the missing letter in this series:

B C D E I K O X

See answer 83.

2 Which letter can complete this series:

A H I M O U V W X Y

See answer 47.

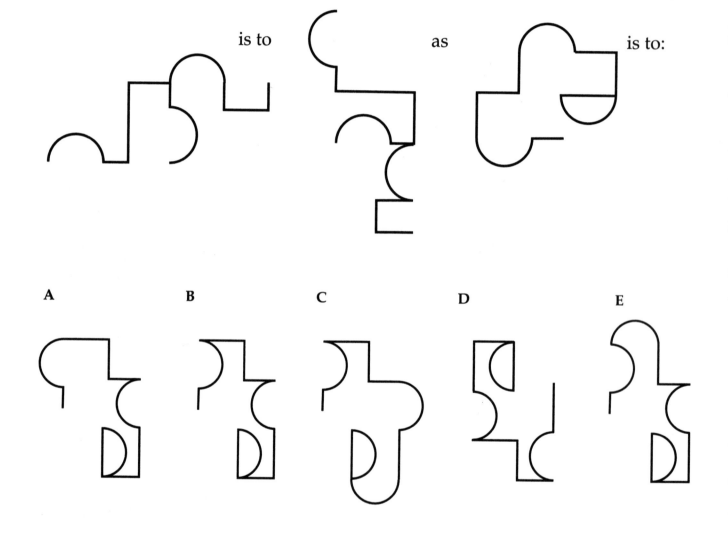

See answer 41.

1 You are walking down the road when suddenly there is a terrific bang. A bomb has exploded. You look round and, to your horror, see a scene of dreadful carnage with bodies lying all over the road. Miraculously, though you are only a few feet away, you are completely unscathed. How could this be?

See answer 55.

2 A man with a phobia about doctors notices a large black growth has appeared on his head. Even though he has no medical or surgical experience he manages successfully to remove the growth. How?

See answer 221.

3 Why do English men use more soap than Irish men (without being noticeably cleaner)?

See answer 102.

4 A saloon gambler produces three cards and challenges the other customers to a little wager. The first card is red on both sides, the second is red on one side and white on the other and the third is white on both sides. Then he places a card on the table with the red side showing and said, 'This can't be the white/white card so the other side must be red or white. That makes it an even money bet. I'll bet $10 against your $10 on the colour of the other side.' What are the true odds of the gambler winning?

See answer 38.

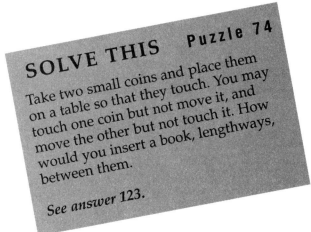

SOLVE THIS   Puzzle 74

Take two small coins and place them on a table so that they touch. You may touch one coin but not move it, and move the other but not touch it. How would you insert a book, lengthways, between them.

See answer 123.

Sam Slick's uncle was always bragging about his exploits in the war. One day he told me how, as a young captain in the campaign in Normandy, he led his battalion against a vastly superior enemy force and completely routed them. Naturally the hero was decorated for his efforts. Delighted for once to have caught the old devil out Sam shouted, 'Uncle, that's a whopper!' Sam knew little about the war so how could he tell?

See answer 12.

How much is the question mark worth?

See answer 94.

The values of the segments are 3 consecutive numbers under 10. The blank is worth 7 and the sum of the segments equals 50. What do the black and speckled segments equal?

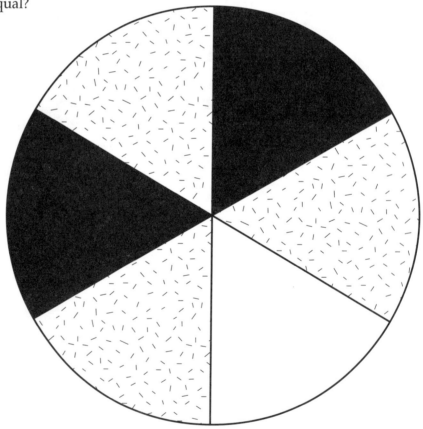

See answer 58.

How much is the question mark worth?

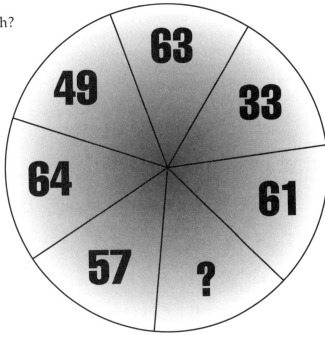

See answer 29.

What letter does the question mark represent ?

5	KP	7
X ?		U B
6	O G	8

See answer 114.

You have become lost in London. Use the grid to locate the following well-known places. Names may be spelt in any direction, not necessarily in a straight line.

CHARING CROSS

COVENT GARDEN

SOHO

WHITEHALL

HYDE PARK

KINGS CROSS

GOLDEN SQUARE

TRAFALGAR SQUARE

PICCADILLY CIRCUS

REGENT'S PARK ZOO

TOWER OF LONDON

BUCKINGHAM PALACE

WESTMINSTER

CHELSEA

KNIGHTSBRIDGE

WATERLOO

See answer 166.

A	N	O	W	T	H	W	E	S	T	M	I	N	S	T	E	R	E	K	R
B	C	L	A	Q	P	O	D	Y	U	P	D	P	Z	Z	L	E	F	I	I
N	I	H	T	S	I	H	E	S	T	I	Y	U	U	A	R	E	D	N	W
H	A	E	E	C	N	A	R	E	T	L	H	C	E	O	S	E	P	G	E
O	P	R	R	L	C	E	G	O	L	I	N	G	I	T	S	O	C	S	O
U	I	G	L	O	O	A	H	I	U	W	P	S	R	O	M	R	E	C	C
A	S	N	H	T	H	A	D	T	S	H	W	H	C	U	S	A	A	R	T
I	G	C	W	A	S	O	H	O	N	I	T	T	O	K	O	H	G	O	E
R	E	I	R	S	I	M	L	J	G	T	I	N	G	N	W	L	M	S	Y
G	U	T	O	O	T	N	E	D	G	E	H	A	L	L	A	U	N	S	T
A	N	S	D	W	S	S	H	R	T	A	T	D	O	F	B	O	G	K	I
G	O	L	D	E	N	E	T	A	O	F	O	R	A	M	D	Y	N	T	R
O	L	E	B	S	O	U	K	G	W	E	Y	R	U	N	C	K	A	I	L
U	B	A	Q	S	L	R	T	T	E	L	T	F	O	A	P	L	G	H	T
E	I	U	F	Y	A	O	N	U	R	O	F	L	L	A	M	C	A	N	S
R	A	R	O	P	A	E	E	T	H	S	T	A	Y	A	U	E	A	B	Y
E	A	D	E	L	V	R	L	G	I	N	C	S	H	O	R	L	R	L	A
R	A	D	M	O	R	A	L	E	E	E	C	G	P	A	R	I	E	T	Y
E	Y	S	C	A	T	B	U	C	K	I	N	W	H	A	D	Y	N	O	U
H	N	O	T	C	H	E	L	S	E	A	J	O	E	G	R	K	Z	O	O

Mario Peroni, the world famous musician, left his studio window open only to find that the wind had destroyed his precious sheet music. Can you put together the names of 10 famous composers from the pieces shown here?

BAR PU C RACH MAN

IUS MAH EL ZART

SKY SCHU RIM SIB

KOR BERT CELL USMO

DE SAKOV OV CI

NI LER IN

TOK LI PUR

See answer 35.

Which comes next in the sequence?

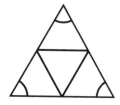  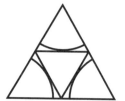 

A   B   C   D   E

  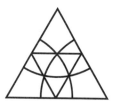 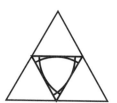 

See answer 207.

1 What can you spend but never buy?

See answer 85.

2 Why are man-hole covers so often round?

See answer 169.

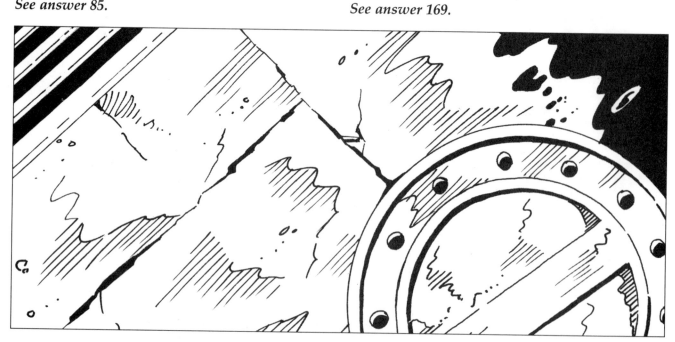

1 A deaf man noticed a bather taking an early morning dip. Just then he saw the tell-tale dorsal fin of a shark approach. In what way could he communicate with the swimmer?

See answer 126.

2 What is the difference between a north wind and a north road?

See answer 37.

1 Use six matches to form four equilateral triangles.

See answer 129.

2 Place three matches on top of three wine glasses in such a way that they will support a pile of coins.

See answer 130.

3 Arrange five matches to add up to fourteen.

See answer 131.

4 Lay down 17 matches so that they form six squares as below. Now remove only five matches and leave just three squares.

See answer 133.

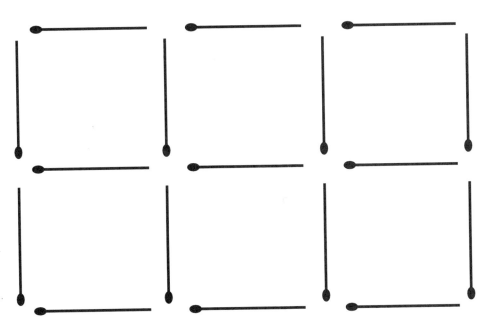

1 On the back seat of a car lies a spirit level. When the car goes round a sharp bend which way will the bubble in the level move, in towards the curb or out towards the middle of the road?

See answer 89.

2 A young couple are about to buy a newly built house. The builder is showing them round and has just reached the bedrooms when he excuses himself and goes to look out the window. With a look of exasperation he flings the window open and yells, 'Green side up, Charlie! Green side up!' He turns back and smiling apologetically explains that he has recently taken on a new lad who is none too bright. Several times during the conversation he flings the window open and shouts the same message to Charlie, but what does it mean?

See answer 8.

3 The little Scots island of Moray boasts the grandly titled Bridge Over the Atlantic (the locals gloss over the fact that, at this point, the Atlantic is only a few feet wide). The bridge is only single track and every morning McLeod the postman drives his van at breakneck speed over the bridge and on to the island. However, every morning Campbell the milkman, who has finished his round, drives his van at similar speed across the bridge as he leaves the island. Neither could ever bring himself to give way so why is there never an accident?

See answer 91.

4 Which is the odd one out: grandfather, sibling, brother-in-law, mother, aunt?

See answer 162.

5 Why is 31 June of such great importance to the islanders of Minki?

See answer 20.

6 Where would you find a system of tunnels 60,000 miles long?

See answer 96.

This is statement which was made at a conference on global warming. 'I can prove that all this fuss about greenhouse gases is nonsense,' stated the scientist boldly. 'Every year the global temperature rises slightly and this is followed about five months later by a rise in the amount of carbon dioxide in the atmosphere. Therefore the carbon dioxide cannot be responsible for the rise in temperature.' Was his logic correct?

See answer 25.

This time you have missed your way in New York. However, the famous places can be located by careful study of the grid. They may be spelt in any direction, not necessarily in a straight line.

BROOKLYN
CITY HALL
UN HQ

LINCOLN CENTER
GREENWICH VILLAGE
FLATIRON BUILDING

BRONX
GRAMERCY PARK
YANKEE STADIUM
HARLEM
LITTLE ITALY
MADISON SQUARE GARDEN

SOHO
CARNEGIE HALL
TIMES SQUARE
CHINA TOWN
GUGGENHEIM

See answer 167.

G	A	C	H	I	N	A	T	O	W	N	U	L	H	V	R	E	G	S	O
Z	R	B	L	T	N	O	S	I	D	A	M	I	Y	X	N	N	O	I	P
R	T	E	U	A	C	S	B	L	D	F	G	T	H	R	T	R	K	M	E
A	L	G	E	P	R	Q	Q	S	A	C	T	T	A	V	Z	Y	X	A	H
R	I	B	Q	N	Z	N	O	U	P	R	C	L	A	C	B	A	L	A	A
S	N	K	A	C	W	R	A	M	A	B	R	E	I	T	A	L	Y	I	L
D	C	G	E	L	E	I	O	N	D	R	O	N	N	O	T	T	I	L	N
G	O	H	A	T	M	N	C	E	W	C	E	T	A	H	S	T	L	U	E
S	L	W	N	A	V	E	S	H	E	Y	G	I	T	H	A	I	S	N	I
S	N	E	A	P	A	I	V	M	N	A	I	M	N	T	H	R	E	H	A
R	C	S	E	G	E	I	I	T	R	T	I	E	S	G	M	O	L	Q	N
C	I	T	Y	E	L	E	Y	O	D	E	N	S	Q	U	A	R	E	E	U
L	L	A	H	L	H	T	O	F	L	A	Y	T	A	D	I	U	M	R	M
L	T	O	A	N	B	R	O	N	X	C	S	P	A	R	K	N	I	S	L
I	K	G	E	E	G	E	T	T	R	I	E	E	K	N	A	Y	N	G	B
L	E	S	O	G	O	D	F	E	R	O	M	L	A	S	T	R	O	O	N
E	I	T	O	G	A	T	M	E	W	R	F	I	A	T	I	I	N	N	G
T	H	H	E	U	S	A	E	B	L	O	I	N	G	T	P	U	Z	B	Z
L	O	E	S	G	R	A	L	D	T	H	E	G	N	I	D	L	I	U	T
T	I	M	E	G	I	T	B	R	O	O	K	L	Y	N	I	S	A	P	A

Match the first name with the surname of these nine famous actors and actresses.

PAUL

NASTASSJA

DEMI

JACOBI

ROBERTS

HUSTON

RYDER

DEREK

HOFFMAN

ARNOLD

MOORE

JULIA

KINSKI

NEWMAN

WINONA

ANJELICA

DUSTIN

SCHWARZENEGGER

See answer 180.

BRAIN TWISTERS
Puzzle 90

Which is the odd one out?

A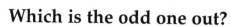

B

C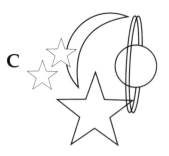

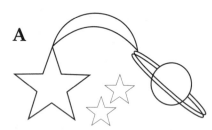

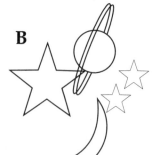

D

E

See answer 208.

52

1 Put down 24 matches to make a three by three grid of squares. Now remove 8 matches to leave only two squares.

See answer 134.

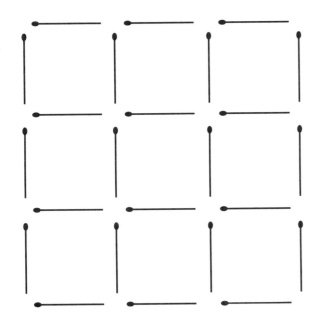

2 Most match puzzles require only some ingenuity and a little mathematical skill, but this one needs a large dollop of both.

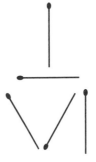

This makes the fraction one sixth. Now add one match so that the result is 1.

See answer 135.

3 Form three squares and two triangles with nine matches.

See answer 136.

1 Farmer Blastem has one of those gas-fuelled bird scaring machines. It lets off an alarming bang once a minute. If he sets it going so that the first bang takes place at 6am, how many times will it have gone off by 7am?

See answer 101.

2 William and Alan are playing with a small plastic ball when it falls down a hole. They find that, no matter how hard they try there is not enough room to get their fingers round the ball to pull it out. 'My dad will kill me,' moans William. 'That ball was a present.' 'Don't worry,' replied his friend, 'there is one sure way to get the ball out.' What did he do?

See answer 57.

1 Another strange but true story. The parish clerk of a Cambridgeshire village received a small parcel from Germany addressed to Mr Alfred White. She checked the telephone directory but could find no one listed under that name. However, when she enquired at the local pub she was told by some of the village old timers that there had been an Alfred White and that, after World War 2, he had married a German girl and settled in Frankfurt. What was in the parcel?

See answer 87.

2 Two little boys come out of a movie. 'I liked the bit where that dinosaur ate all those cave men,' said one. 'Rubbish,' replied his friend, 'it couldn't do it.' 'But that was Tyrannosaurus Rex the most fearsome reptile in the history of the world! Of course it could eat a few lousy cave men.' 'Oh no it couldn't,' insisted his friend with maddening superiority. Who was right?

See answer 98.

3 Dan looked bleakly at the water pump in his car. Kaput! 'I haven't had it more than a couple of years,' he complained to his friend Al. 'You know,' said Al, 'I've got a pump that's lasted 30 years already and I reckon it will keep going for at least twice that long.' Dan was incredulous but Al stuck to his story. What did he mean?

See answer 214.

When the author was a child in Scotland school kids would inflict the following riddle on each other: 'Constantinople is a very big word and if you can't spell it you're a very big dunce!' What was the catch?
See answer 76.

Five couples, each living in a different New York borough, got divorced; and each person then married a partner from one of the other couples. After the change-round no one still lived in the borough where he or she lived before divorcing (i.e., they all moved house). Who is/was married to whom now/previously and where do/did they live? Here are some clues:

1. Mrs Ford (as she is now) lives in the Bronx. Her former husband is Dick, and she isn't Donna.

2. Anna (previously Mrs Smith from Queens) married Joan's former husband and now lives in Brooklyn.

3. Betsy Jones (her current name) was originally from Staten Island; and Jim came from Manhattan before divorcing.

4. Dave and Joan Martin haven't made their new home on Staten Island; and Bobby wasn't the present Mrs Martin's former husband.

Fill in the tables to help you to get the answer.

See answer 171.

Man's New Home   Man's Old Home

	Anna	Betsy	Donna	Joan	Mary	Bronx	Brooklyn	Manhattan	Queens	Staten Island	Bronx	Brooklyn	Manhattan	Queens	Staten Island
Bobby Ford															
Dick Jones																
Jim Lewis																
Dave Martin																
Hank Smith																
Bronx																
Brooklyn																
Manhattan																
Queens																
Staten Island																
Bronx																
Brooklyn																
Manhattan																
Queens																
Staten Island																
Bobby Ford																
Dick Jones																
Jim Lewis																
Dave Martin																
Hank Smith																

Woman's Old Home

Woman's New Home

Woman's Ex-Husband

	Ex-Wife	Ex-Home	New Wife	New Home
Bobby Ford				
Dick Jones				
Jim Lewis				
Dave Martin				
Hank Smith				

What comes next in the sequence?

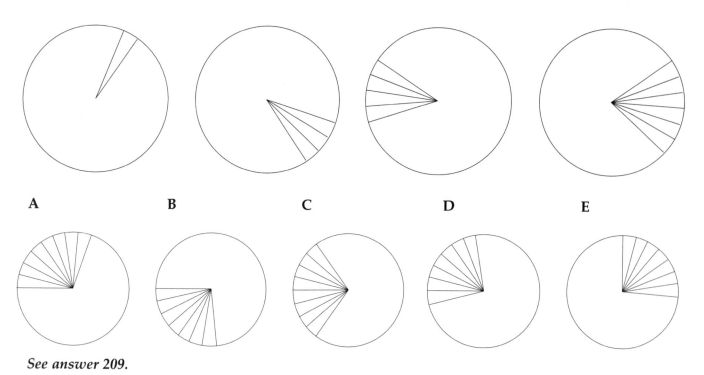

A   B   C   D   E

See answer 209.

What comes next in the sequence?

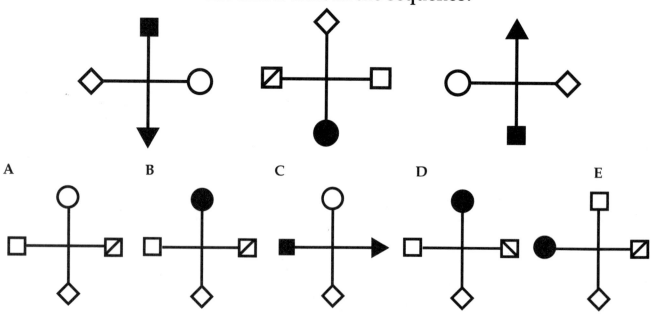

A   B   C   D   E

See answer 99.

Here's a challenge! Make the sum below work without moving any matches at all.

See answer 148.

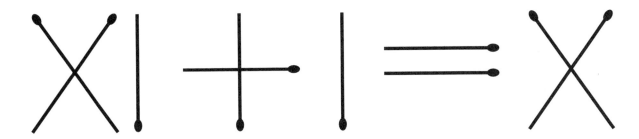

Here is a long division sum showing all the working and the result. What could be simpler? The sum works out exactly with no remainder. The slight complication is that all the numbers have been replaced with letters on a random basis. However, one letter always represents the same number. Can you reconstruct the original sum?

See answer 112.

```
              CDEFG
        AB | ADGAAHD
             AJK
             AKA
             AAG
              FA
              JF
             AGH
             AEE
              FD
```

Look at the triangles below. What geometrical shape should logically be placed in the fourth triangle?

See answer 111.

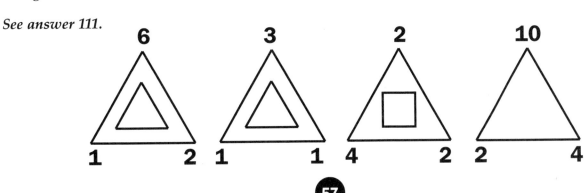

This is a puzzle which is much more fun if you try it on an unsuspecting victim. Take a conical wine glass and two coins, one larger than the other. Place the small coin in the glass first and then the larger. Both coins should lie horizontally with a space between them. You will have to experiment with coins and glasses until you get a combination which will work. Now challenge your victim to remove the smaller coin without touching either of the coins or the glass. If you are particularly sadistic you may even leave a small magnet lying nearby (this will be of no use whatever but may give your victim a considerable amount of frustration trying to work out how to use it). Can you guess how to extract the small coin?

See answer 139.

Which cube below can be made using the diagram on the right:

See answer 189.

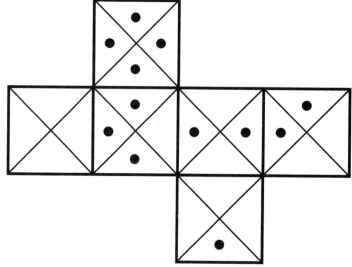

A   B   C   D   E

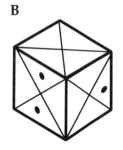

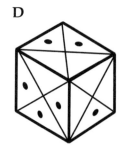
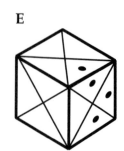

The annual International Championship cross-country is always a close-run race. This year was no exception with five athletes from various countries having fought their way through to the finals. The last race was to be held over a 10-mile course as shown in the diagram. The race itself was split into four legs, with timekeepers at the end of each leg to record the runners' times. The contestants race from the start A to the end of the first leg at post B, and then on to C and D, finally the sprint across the shortest leg to finish at E. The distances in miles of each of these legs is shown on the course diagram, while the runners' average speeds have been worked out for each leg and then flashed on to the electronic scoreboard, represented in feet per second. (There are 5,280 feet in one mile).

The scoreboard is shown below as it appeared at the end of the race, with all the runners' speeds

displayed. Obviously, the first runner past the finishing post won the race. Can you work out their respective times and thus the correct finishing order?

Times in feet/second

RUNNER

	A-B	B-C	C-D	D-E
John	14	12.5	11	13.75
Pierre	13.75	15	8	18.75
Pedro	15	12	8.25	22
Bruce	13	16	8.75	16.5
Ivan	12.75	14	9.75	17.5

See answer 172.

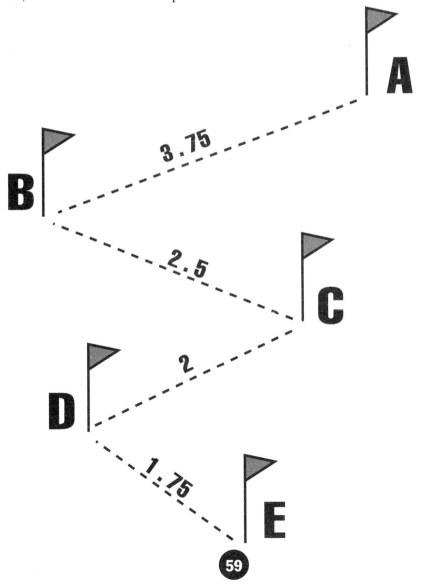

Which is the odd one out?

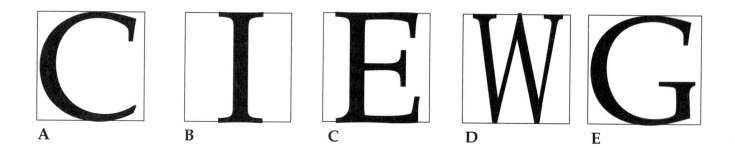

A B C D E

See answer 61.

Which is the odd one out?

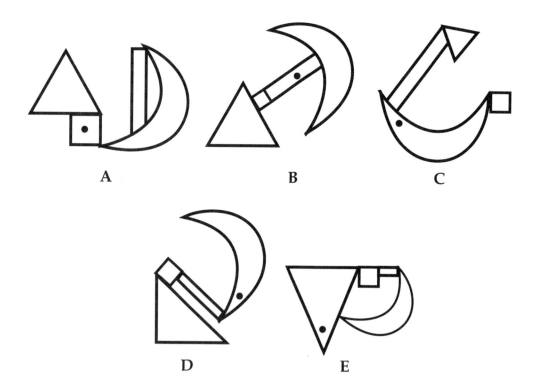

A B C

D E

See answer 216.

1 Queens' College, Cambridge, has a mathematical bridge designed by Sir Isaac Newton. The idea was that all the timbers fitted together without the use of nails, glue or other artificial aids. It worked perfectly until some bright spark decided to take it to bits for refurbishment. They eventually got it back together but only by using hefty metal bolts to hold it. Could you design a similar bridge using a couple of dozen matchsticks? Your bridge need have no sides, it will be a flat object which can be raised in the middle so that it bends without breaking.

See answer 140.

2 How would you make a tower of twenty matchboxes which you could hold in one hand without it falling over. No glue, sticky tape, etc, is allowed - just guile, cunning and general sneakiness!

See answer 137.

3 Take a matchbox and pull it apart. Then put the parts together as shown in the diagram. Now turn the whole thing upside down. You may hold the case by a finger and thumb only but you must not touch the tray at all.

See answer 138.

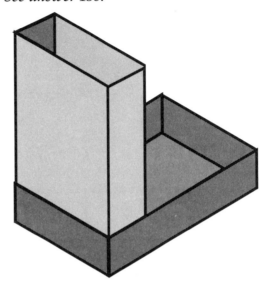

1 This one is a true story. A racing cyclist came off his bike at speed, fell awkwardly and broke nearly all the bones in his right hand. After hospital treatment the hand was much improved and, one day, a consultant invited a group of students to consider the case. 'This man,' he said, 'is not a professional cyclist. He works as a graphic designer. How long after the accident do you think he was able to return to work?' The students examined x-rays of the hand taken just after the accident and gave a variety of opinions. What would your answer have been?

See answer 92.

2 Many authors have written entertainingly about time travel but what would actually happen if you could be taken out of time for, say, five seconds and then returned to exactly the same spot?

See answer 72.

The numbers in this calculation have been replaced by letters. All the numbers from 0-9 have been used, and by telling you that R=2 we hope to have given you enough information to keep you down to one solution. Each letter represents the same number every time it appears. Can you work out the original calculation?

See answer 173.

QR	÷	S	x	T	=	UV
−		−		+		÷
WX	+	Y	−	U	=	RV

TU ÷ Z ÷ S = R

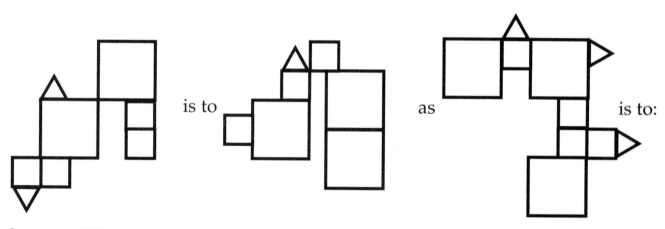

is to ... as ... is to:

See answer 210.

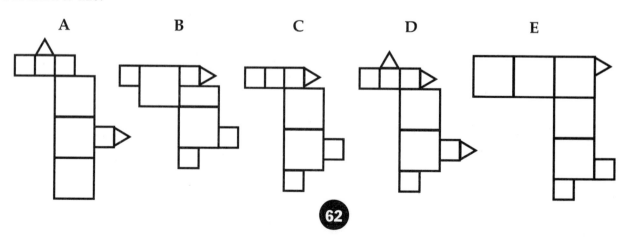

A   B   C   D   E

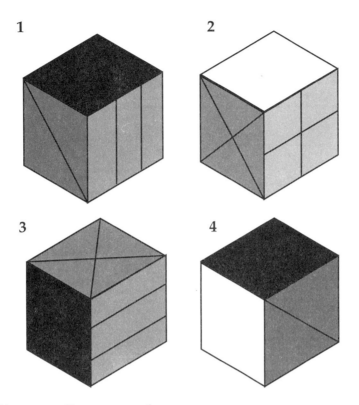

Have a look at these diagrams. Can you work out what is opposite the blank face of cube number 4?

See answer 67.

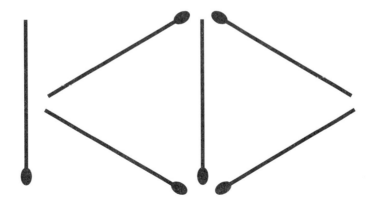

Lay six matches in a fish pattern as above: Now try to make eight equilateral triangles by moving three matches.

See answer 142.

Use six straight lines to divide the diagram into seven sections containing 1, 2, 3, 4, 5, 6, and 7 stars respectively. The lines always touch one edge of the box, but not necessarily two.

See answer 179.

Which of the following completes a diamond when fitted with the diagram below:

See answer 223.

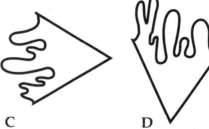

A   B

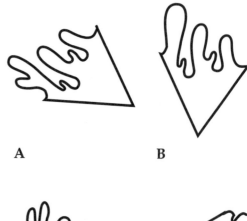

C   D   E

DEAD END

E-MAIL MESSAGE

From: Chief of Police O'Malley
To: Robotic Tracer XJ -256   **Location:** New York
Dateline: 4 August 2210   **Security Code:** 10

Yesterday evening at 10pm the President's daughter was kidnapped. A news blackout was immediately enforced but, in spite of the best efforts of all law enforcement agencies, no trace was found. In the last hour a message was received from the kidnapper. A transcript follows.

"My name is Alan Timms and, until recently, I worked as a scientist in the Department of Defense. In spite of my genius and the many brilliant ideas that I have offered for the defense of this country I have never received the recognition that was my due. Again and again I have been passed over in favor of some blue-eyed boy with a gift for self advancement. Six months ago I discovered that I was dying. So I made a decision. If I was not to go down in history as one of the world's great scientists, then I would be the greatest criminal of all time. I have now kidnapped the President's daughter. There is no need to look for her, she is to be found in a deserted office block marked on the map you will find with this note. I am with her. However, before you come blundering in here with your police and your National Guard, there are things you should know. The girl is locked inside a machine of my own devising. She is floating in a pressurised bath of nutrients and can safely remain in suspension for as long as necessary.

However, if any attempt is made to release her a cocktail of deadly nerve gases will be introduced into the chamber and she will die an agonising death right in front of your eyes. I have devised a little game and, if you want the girl back, you will agree to play it. All around New York I have hidden a series of clues. You will select an agent to follow my trail and solve every riddle I have set. If your agent can follow the correct path and find the correct code you will be able to open the machine and release the girl. But you will have to be fast. From the moment your agent starts you have only two hours."

Tracer XJ-256, the map he mentions can be viewed on your telescreen. As you solve each puzzle you will be given the location of the next. Your country depends on you. Good luck.

1 POLICE STATION

All the objects in this grid have a numerical value. The totals of the values for each row, column and one of the diagonals have been inserted. One figure is missing and it is up to you to find it. When you have the solution subtract 44 and then go to the location of that number.

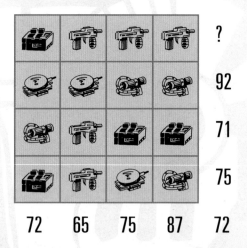

2 EAST VILLAGE

You are supplied with three darts which you throw at the board. Assume that each time you throw them all the darts hit the board. How many different ways are there of scoring 12? When you have the answer add 23 and go to that location.

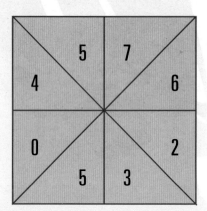

3 BATTERY PARK

This is a road map of part of New York City. You can see the routes taken by four drivers A, B, C, D. The side of each square is one mile long. The speed of driver A is 20 mph. Driver B drives at 22 mph. Driver C drives at 25 mph. Driver D drives at 27 mph. Which car(s) reach a shaded circle first and in what time? When you have the time in minutes subtract 13 and go to the location of that number.

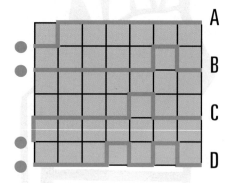

4 EMPIRE STATE

BUILDING

The figures in the diagram are linked in some way. Find the figure which should go in the middle of the third triangle. When you have it add 18 and go to the location of that number.

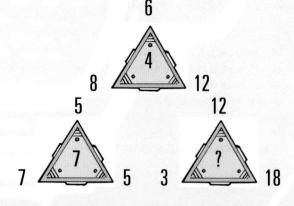

5 YANKEE STADIUM

Look at the three sets of scales. Each object has a certain weight. Which object is needed to balance the last set of scales?

If your answer is a circle, go to location **22**   If your answer is a triangle, go to location **9**
If your answer is a rectangle, go to location **13**   If your answer is a square, go to location **10**

6 GRAND CENTRAL STATION

This signpost shows you the distances to a number of New York locations. The distances shown are calculated from numerical values placed upon the letters in each name. Find the distance to Grand Central Station. When you know the answer subtract 47 and go to the location of that number.

RIVERSIDE PARK	47
TIMES SQUARE	39
HARLEM	22
GRAND CENTRAL STATION	?

7 STATUE OF LIBERTY

The numbers around the squares are linked in some way. Find the correct number to go in the middle of the third square. When you have it subtract 134 and go to the location of the number you now have.

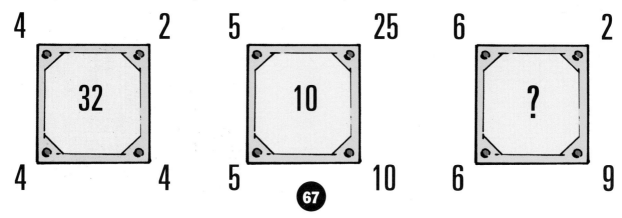

8 FIREARMS COMPLEX

The numbers on the diagram have a relationship to each other. Can you find out what it is and thus fill in the missing number? When you have done it subtract 83 and go to the next location.

```
   10   6 | 5    6
11    16 | 5       7
 8  27   |     63  8
---------+---------
 9  56   |     ?   9
    30   | 60
 7       |         3
    5    1 | 8    2
```

9 ROCKEFELLER CENTER

All the objects in this diagram have a numerical value. Find the number which will correctly replace the question mark. When you have it divide it by 4. The result will take you to the next location.

				?
				59
				78
				57
77	73	44	60	73

10 SOHO

Find the missing letter in this series. If your answer is G, go to 2. If your answer is H, go to 11. If your answer is K, go to 26. If your answer is L, go to 35.

C F H ? M

Flip this figure over and rotate it. Which of the figures below do you get? If your answer is A, go to 21. If your answer is B, go to 12. If your answer is C, go to 30. If your answer is D, go to 6.

The numbers you see here are related in some way. Crack the logic and find the missing number. When you have it subtract 30 and go to your next location.

13 BROOKLYN BRIDGE

Here is a signpost in which the distances are all related to the letters used. Find the distance to China Town, subtract 29, and continue to the next location.

SOHO	18
TRIBECA	29
LITTLE ITALY	42
CHINA TOWN	?

14 MANHATTAN

These Roman numerals are connected by some strange logic. Find the missing one, add XVI, and go on to the next location.

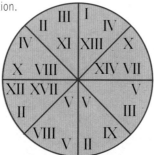

15 HARLEM

This wall is covered with graffiti. The words are connected in some kind of series. Who does Oliver love? If you think it's Lauren, go to location 16. If you think it's Nicole, go to location 3. If you think it's Latoya, go to location 29. If you think it's Urania, go to location 10. If you think it's Kimberley, go to location 26.

Aaron ♥ Crystal

Franco ♥ Jessica

Oliver ♥

Lauren, Nicole, Latoya, Urania, Kimberley.

16 AIRPORT

Find the missing number. When you have it add 28 and continue on your way.

3	7	5	5
6	6	6	2
7	11	1	1
8	3	4	?

17 NATIONAL HEALTH COMPLEX

These letters are an anagram of a place in New York. Unscramble the words and look up the number of that place on the map. Subtract 23 and go to a new location.

S N Y B T I O G K H R H E L O

18 MAXIMUM SECURITY PRISON

Try to find the logic which connects these numbers. When you find the missing one subtract 135 and go to your new location.

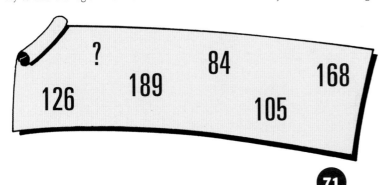

? 84 168 126 189 105

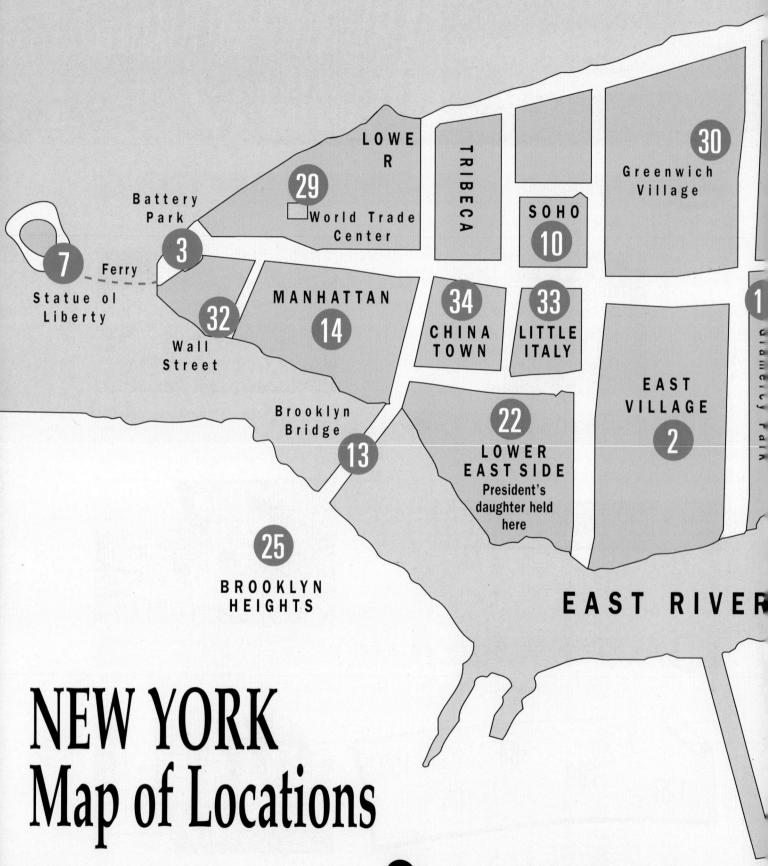

HUDSON

LOWER

29

Battery Park

3

7

Ferry

Statue of Liberty

32

Wall Street

MANHATTAN

14

World Trade Center

TRIBECA

SOHO

10

34

CHINA TOWN

33

LITTLE ITALY

30

Greenwich Village

1

Gramercy Park

EAST VILLAGE

2

Brooklyn Bridge

13

22

LOWER EAST SIDE
President's daughter held here

25

BROOKLYN HEIGHTS

EAST RIVER

NEW YORK
Map of Locations

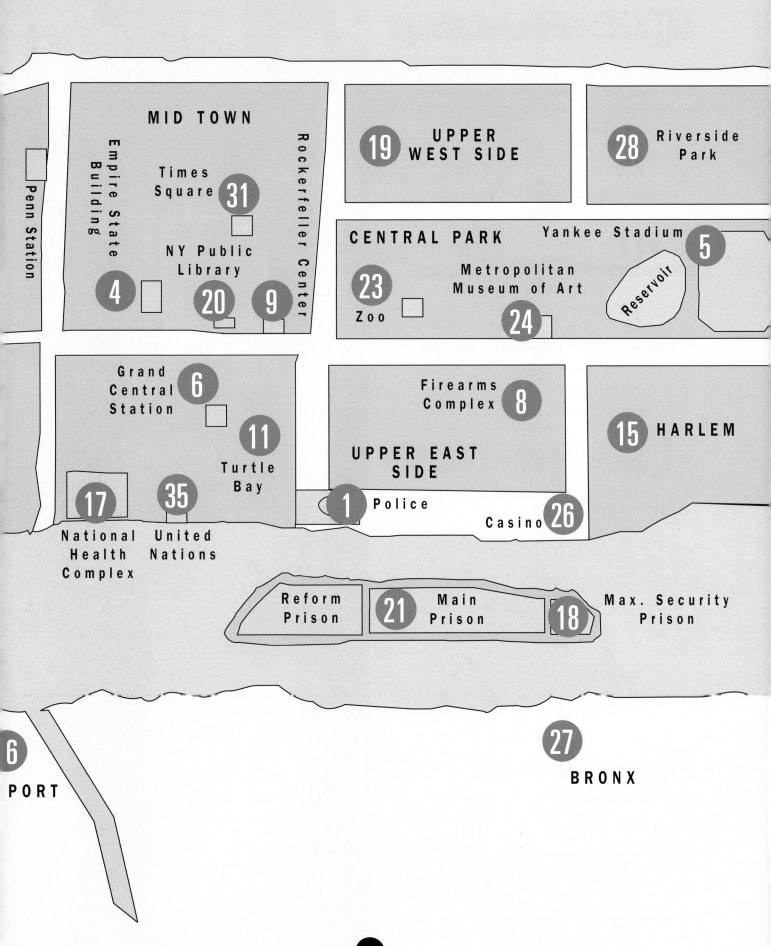

MID TOWN

Empire State Building

Times Square **31**

Rockerfeller Center

NY Public Library

Penn Station

4

20

9

19 UPPER WEST SIDE

28 Riverside Park

CENTRAL PARK

Yankee Stadium

5

Reservoir

23

Zoo

Metropolitan Museum of Art

24

Grand Central Station

6

11

Turtle Bay

Firearms Complex **8**

15 HARLEM

UPPER EAST SIDE

1 Police

17

35

National Health Complex

United Nations

26 Casino

Reform Prison

21 Main Prison

18

Max. Security Prison

6

PORT

27

BRONX

19 UPPER WEST SIDE

Look at the scales. Each object has a numerical value. Try to work out which object is needed to balance the last set of scales. If your answer is a circle, go to 14. If your answer is a rectangle, go to 29. If your answer is a triangle. go to 31. If your answer is a square, go to 32.

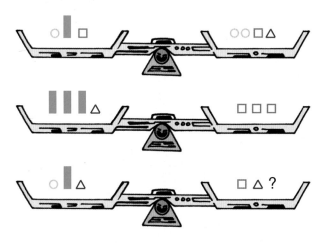

20 N.Y. PUBLIC LIBRARY

Look at the triangles. Work out what the missing figure is, subtract 17 and continue on your way.

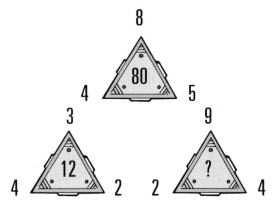

21 MAIN PRISON

Here is another anagram of a New York place name. When you have worked it out look up the number of that place on the map and subtract 6 to get your next location.

EVLGRENG AWHCLEII

22 LOWER EAST SIDE

The numbers surrounding the squares are connected in some way. Work out the logic and supply the missing number. When you have it subtract 14 and find your new destination.

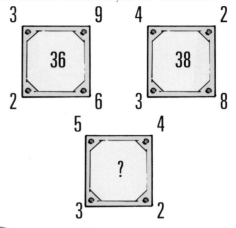

23 ZOO

Again a number is missing. Unravel the logic to find the missing number then subtract 115 and go to the new location.

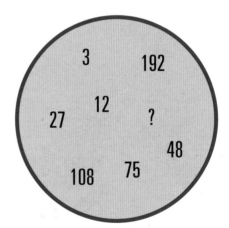

24 METROPOLITAN

MUSEUM OF ART

Here is another number grid. Replace the question mark with a number, add 19 and go to the next location.

8	9	8	6
6	4	7	7
6	8	5	8
9	8	9	?

25 BROOKLYN HEIGHTS

Look at the building facing you. The height of the building opposite, measured in yards, is 2 times the square of 5, multiplied by the square root of 36. When you have the solution subtract 284 and go to the next location.

26 CASINO

You need to choose two figures to complete the pattern. Which do you choose. If your choice is HB, go to location 18. If you choose EF, go to location 29. If you choose AG, go to 25. If you choose DC, go to 15. If you choose DH, go to 16.

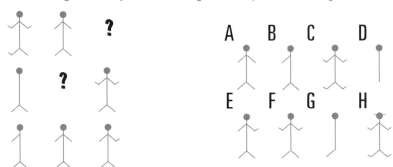

27 BRONX

Find the figure which goes next in the series. If you choose A go to 23. If you choose B, go to 28. If you choose C, go to 13. If you choose D, go to 11.

A   B   C   D

28 RIVERSIDE PARK

Find the missing number. When you have it add 17 and go to the next location.

$$\frac{4 \,|\, 9}{12 \,|\, 3} \qquad \frac{11 \,|\, 8}{22 \,|\, 4} \qquad \frac{7 \,|\, 10}{14 \,|\, ?}$$

29 WORLD TRADE CENTER

Look at the diagrams and find the missing letter. Add 10 to the value of that letter and go to the next location.

G	A	Z	43
F	K	N	13
T	O	P	15
33	72	65	

N	P	R	84
T	Q	C	4
A	V	B	52
53	55	32	

C	J	L	52
I	?	B	53
M	V	D	93
52	65	81	

30 GREENWICH VILLAGE

If a clock takes 5 seconds to strike six, how many seconds will it take to strike 12? Subtract 4 from your answer and continue to the next location.

31 TIMES SQUARE

How many squares of any size are there in this figure? Add 15 and go to the next location.

32 WALL STREET

Your trial has ended. You should now have a list of the location you have visited. Add together all the numbers between locations 24 and 10. Enter this total into the computer and, if it is correct, the President's daughter will be relased. Or will she?

aWhat number is half the value of a third of 102? When you discover the answer, add 1 and go to the location of that number.

34 CHINATOWN

Find the missing number. When you have it, go to that location.

1	2	5	7
47	55	62	11
41	79	71	?
34	29	23	19

35 UN HQ

There is a curious logic to this series. Can you replace the question mark with the final number? (The answer is right before your eyes!) When you have the number, divide it by 2.

5 2 1 7 5 2 4 6 3 3 7 3 8 4 4 3 5 ?

1 Dick is getting dressed for an important dinner party with the boss and his wife. They are outside in the car waiting to take him to the restaurant. He is already running late when suddenly, disaster! There's a power cut. He hasn't yet put on his socks. He knows that in the drawer there are a dozen pairs of black socks and an equal number of navy ones. What is the smallest number of socks he must take out of the drawer to avoid the embarrassment of mismatched socks?

See answer 103.

2 Dave and Anne moved into their new home and then went to the DIY store to make an important purchase. 'How much is one?' asked Dave. '$3,' came the reply. 'What about 20?' 'That'll cost you $6.' 'OK, well we need 2042.' What were Dave and Anne buying and how much did it cost them?

See answer 218.

This is a sum using Roman numerals made out of matches. Move one match to make the sum correct.

See answer 145.

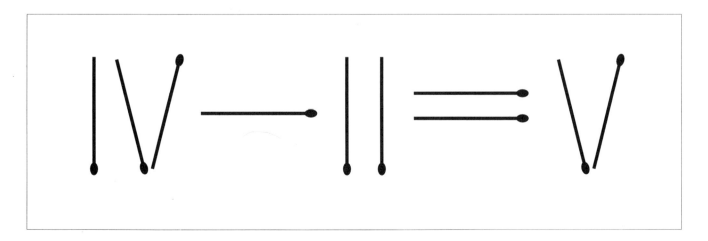

Which one of the five pieces shown correctly fits into the vacant section of the grid?

See answer 175.

Use five straight lines to divide this square into seven sections containing 1, 2, 3, 4, 5, 6, and 7 spots. The lines always touch one edge of the box, but not necessarily two.

See answer 178.

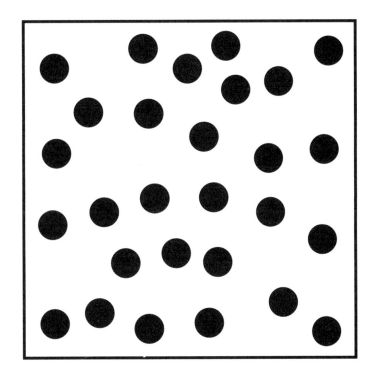

Which is the odd one out?

A   B   C   D   E

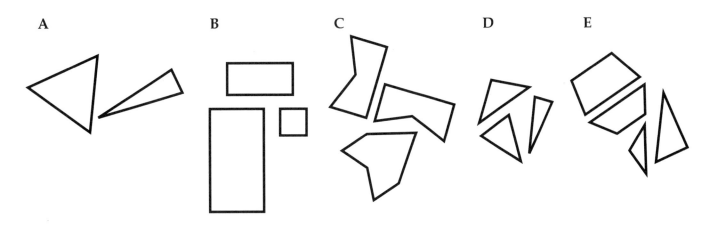

See answer 224.

This simple calculation uses Roman numerals made from matches. Move two matches to make the sum work.

See answer 146.

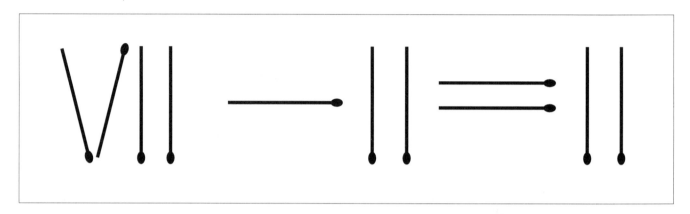

1 Once, in India, a queen owned two horses and used them to help destroy a neighbouring king. There was a hard fought battle in which all the king's men were killed. When the battle was over the victors and the vanquished all lay side by side in the same place. Explain.

See answer 186.

2 What does nobody want but nobody wants to lose?

See answer 220.

Insert one of the four basic mathematical signs in each space to complete the sum, starting from the top. One sign is used twice, the rest once.

+ − X ÷

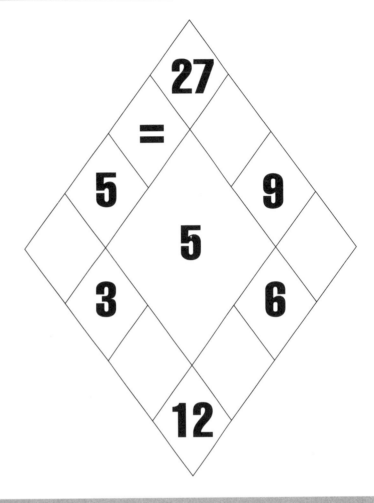

See answer 124.

What letter does the question mark represent ?

10	T N	6
B L		W H
6	? Q	15

See answer 106.

How much is the question mark worth?

See answer 43.

Where should another dot belong?

See answer 79.

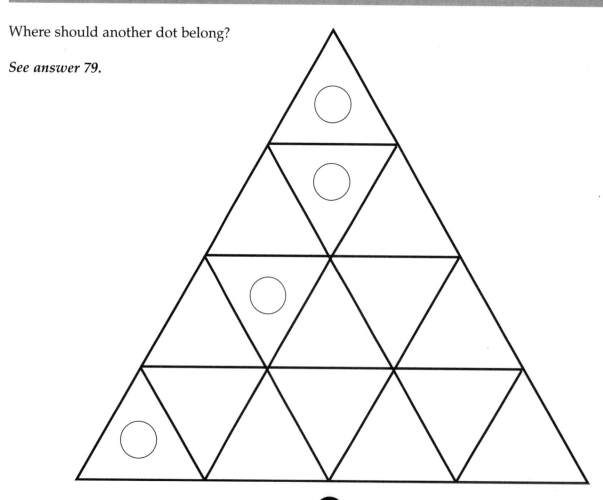

Which one of the five pieces shown correctly fits
into the vacant section of the grid?

See answer 176.

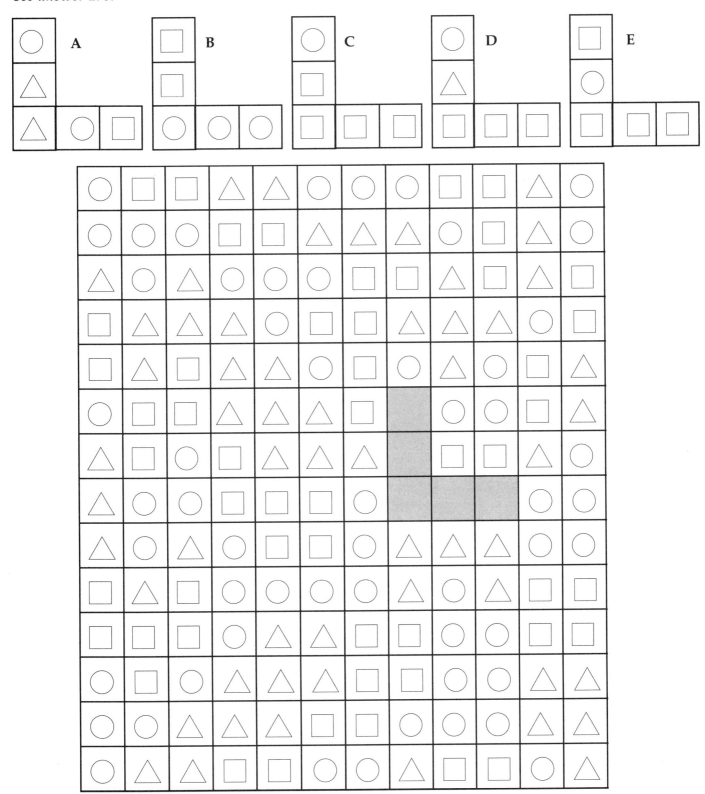

Five colleagues set off for work each day in their vehicles. Work out who drives what and how long they each drive to work.

1. Pauline drives twice as long as the estate car and a quarter of the time that Olivia has to drive in her saloon car.

2. Neville and Pauline drive 60 minutes between them but Neville has five times the travel time as Pauline.

3. The convertible travels half as long as Neville while Lynda takes five times longer than Martin.

4. The sports car has the longest journey and the van has a quarter of the trip of the saloon.

See answer 177.

	Convertible	Estate	Saloon	Sports	Van	5 minutes	10 minutes	25 minutes	40 minutes	50 minutes
Lynda										
Martin										
Neville										
Olivia										
Pauline										
5 minutes						
10 minutes						
25 minutes						
40 minutes						
50 minutes						

Name	Type of Vehicle	Time
Lynda		
Martin		
Neville		
Olivia		
Pauline		

Which is the odd one out?

A

B

C

D

E

See answer 226.

1 Vinyl records are not used much any more but, strangely they still seem perfect for puzzle setters. An old fashioned 78 has a diameter of 12 ins. The outside border is $1/2$ in wide and the distance from there to the central hole is $5^1/2$ ins. If you put the stylus down at the very edge of the playing area how far will the needle have travelled by the time the music stops? You may assume that there are 83 grooves to the inch.

See answer 110.

2 The Bacillus subtilis bacterium reproduces simply by splitting in two. It can do this every 20 minutes. Given perfect conditions how many offspring do you think one organism could produce in eight hours?

See answer 86.

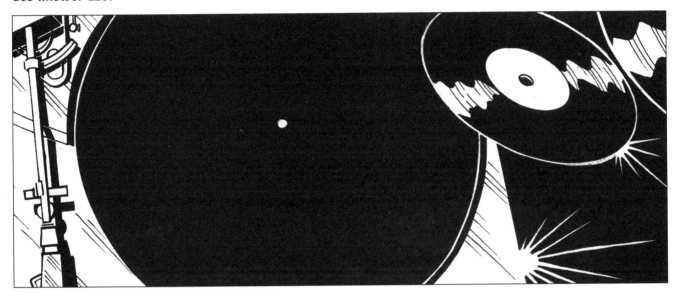

A party of Mensa members was being given a guided tour of the Clocks and Watches Gallery. 'I bet you can't tell me which timepiece has the fewest moving parts,' said the Curator. 'A sundial' bellowed the intellectually gifted ones. 'OK,' said the slightly peeved Curator, 'which timepiece has the most moving parts?' There was a prolonged silence. What was the answer?

See answer 108.

Which of the following cubes below can be made using the flat
one shown here ?

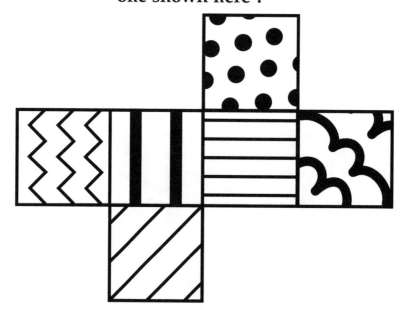

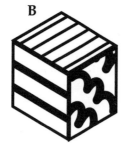
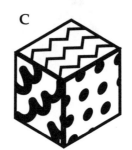
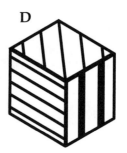
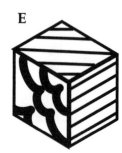

A   B   C   D   E

See answer 21.

Which is the odd one out?

4   **15**   **9**   **12**   **5**
A   B   C   D   E

8   **30**   **18**   **24**   **10**
F   G   H   I   J

See answer 229.

In an orchestra there is something which is neither blown, bowed, plucked or struck but without which the others could not play. What is it?

See answer 128.

Remove three matches from this sum to make the equation correct.

See answer 147.

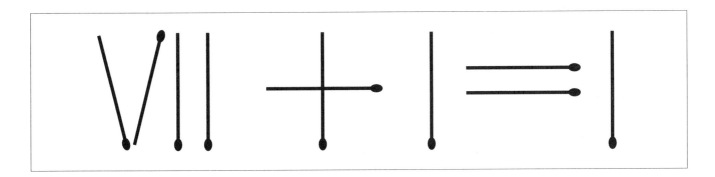

1 How many times can you subtract the number 2 from the number 46?

See answer 24.

2 Eddie has a reputation for being, let's say, economical. There are two girls he's interested in and he has the chance to take them both to the movies. His problem is that he wants a good deal. Will it be cheaper for him to take them both together, or should he take them separately?

See answer 52.

To which of the following can a dot be added to meet the conditions of the drawing on the right?

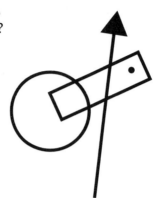

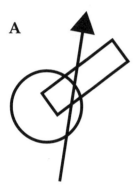    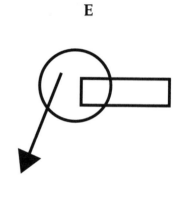

A   B   C   D   E

See answer 212.

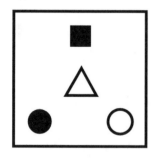 is to 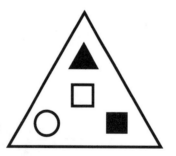 as 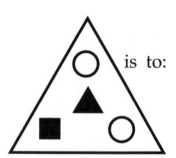 is to:

A   B   C   D   E

See answer 225.

Which one of the five pieces shown correctly fits
into the vacant section of the grid?

See answer 174.

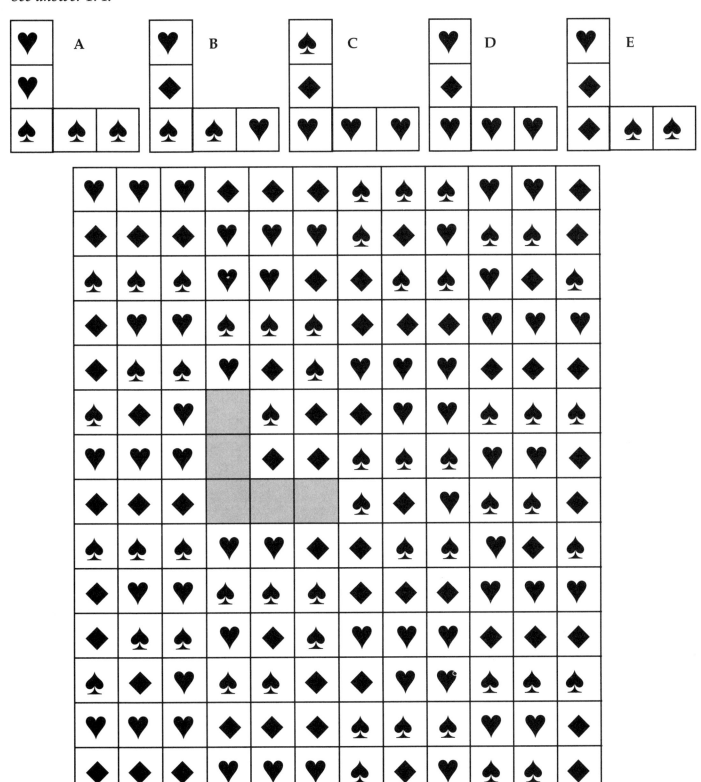

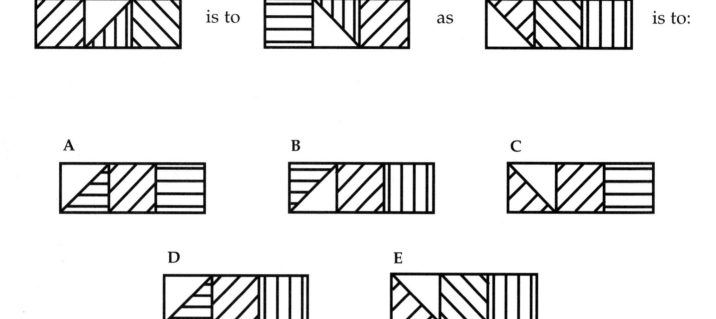

See answer 217.

What comes next in the sequence?

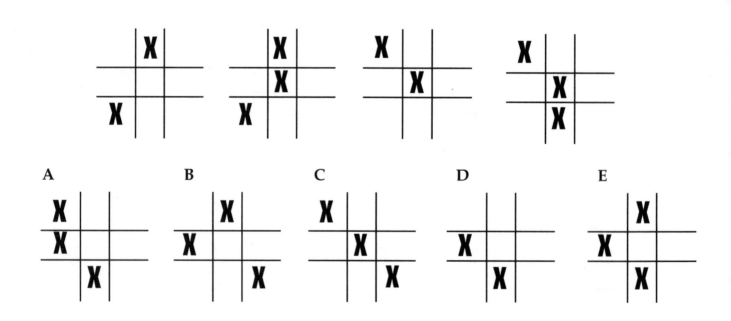

See answer 104.

Which of the following sets of triangles can be used to make a square?

See answer 109.

w is to **n** as **d** is to:

A   B   C   D   E

See answer 75.

What comes next in the following sequence:

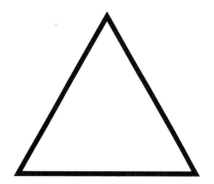
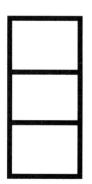
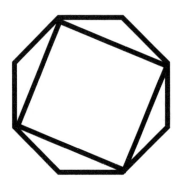

A

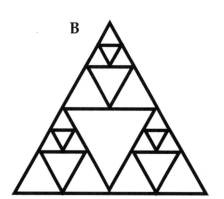

B

C

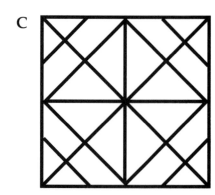

D

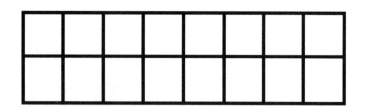

E

See answer 227.

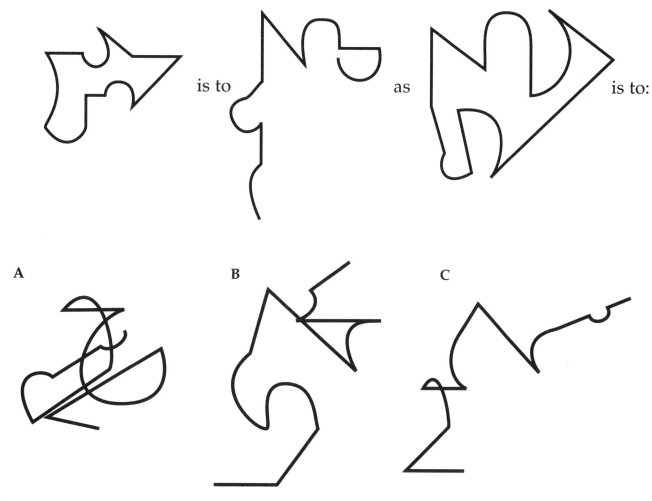

is to ... as ... is to:

A   **B**   **C**

See answer 69.

Which is the odd one out ?

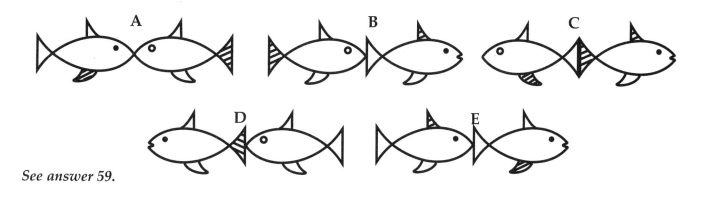

See answer 59.

1 Frieda drove her husband Andy to Chicago airport and watched him climb aboard the 7.15 flight for London. As she arrived home she heard that the 7.15 London flight had crashed on take-off and there were no survivors. Strangely she got on with preparing an evening meal for her and her husband. Why?

See answer 74.

2 Dan and his best friend Dave were out fishing when they noticed a shark circling their dinghy. Whenever they tried to move the boat the shark would barge into it nearly causing it to capsize. 'Never mind,' said Dan, 'if we wait long enough it'll get tired and while it's asleep we can sneak away.' Was this good advice?

See answer 107.

3 Two fathers and two sons went into a bar to have a Friday night drink together. They spent $15. Each spent the same amount. How much did each man spend?

See answer 95.

1 Use 16 matches to make this figure. Now remove four matches to leave four triangles.

See answer 143.

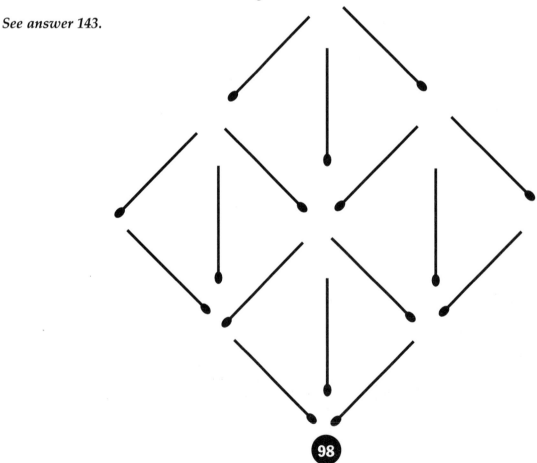

Which of the following fills the gap?

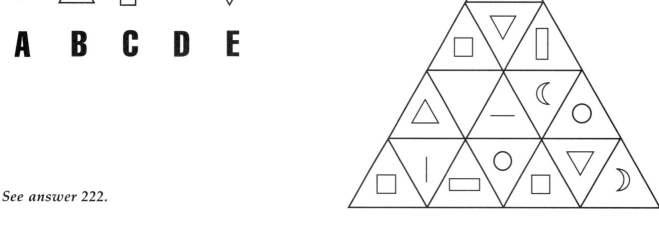

A   B   C   D   E

See answer 222.

How much is the question mark worth?

See answer 73.

How much is the question mark worth?

?	HEY	10
HPZ		ANO
12	IUA	11

See answer 204.

Each pattern is worth a certain value. The values are 3 consecutive odd numbers under 10. With 6 segments, there are 6 values, with the total sum being 16. What is each pattern worth?

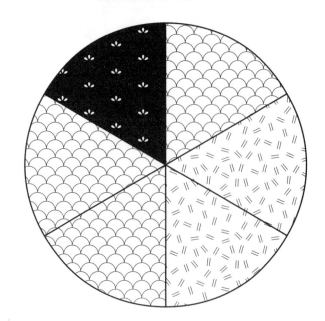

 ?   ?   ?

See answer 105.

Insert one of the four basic mathematical signs in each space to complete the sum, starting from the top. One sign is used twice, the rest once.

+   −   X   ÷

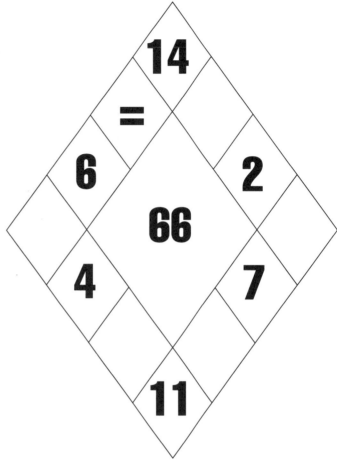

See answer 97.

How much is the question mark worth?

See answer 132.

8	27	19
57	36	34
65	63	?

Insert one of the four basic mathematical signs in each space to complete the sum, starting from the top. One sign is used twice, the rest once. Each letter represents its position in the alphabet, where A = 1 and Z = 26.

See answer 121.

What shape is missing and where should it go?

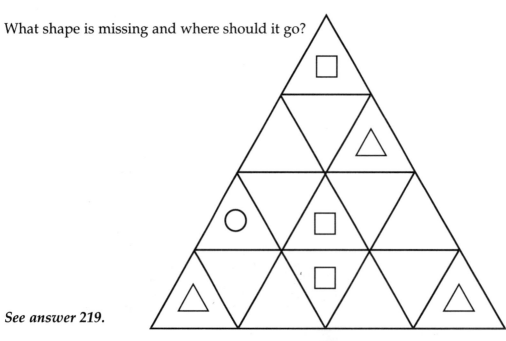

See answer 219.

How much is the question mark worth?

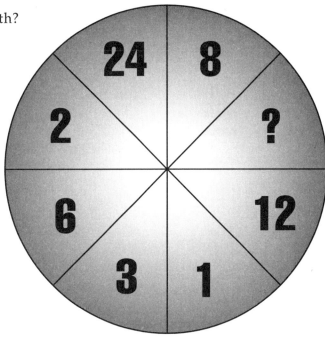

See answer 14.

What letter does the question mark represent ?

?	725	M
1 3 9		4 7 2
I	846	N

See answer 122.

The pattern in each segment is worth either 2, 4, 6 or 8 points. The total value of the circle's 10 segments is 44. What is each pattern worth?

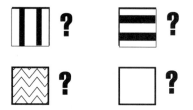 **?**

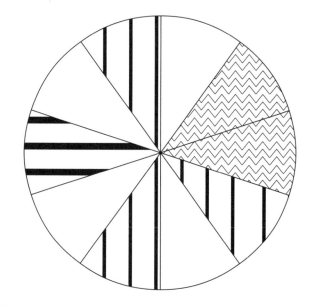

See answer 113.

How much is the question mark worth?

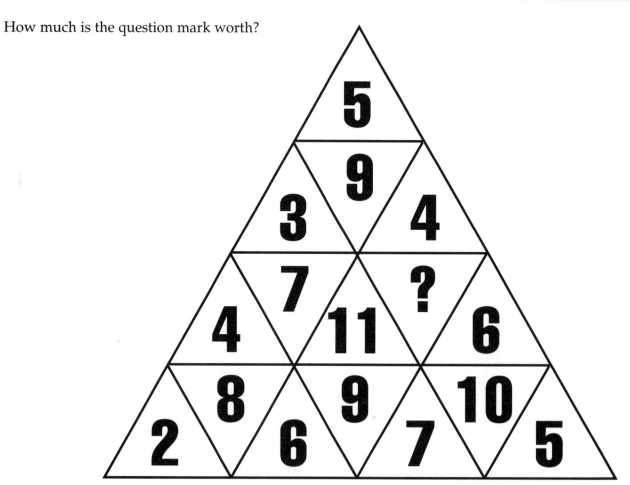

See answer 32.

Insert one of the four basic mathematical
signs in each space to complete the sum,
starting from the top. One sign is used twice,
the rest once.

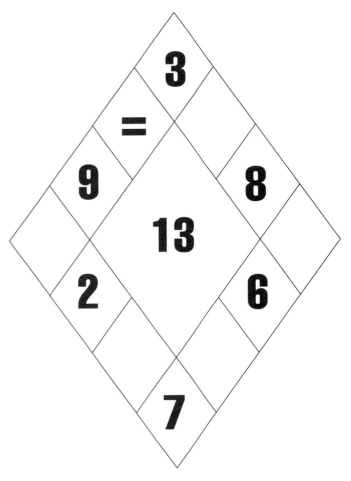

See answer 70.

The values of the patterns are 3 consecutive even
numbers under 10, with the total of 20 being the
sum of the segment values. How much is each
pattern worth?

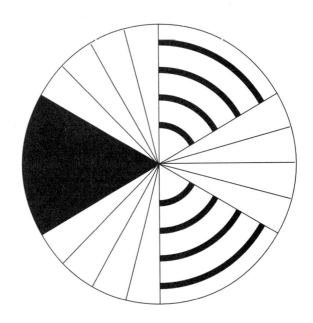

 ?   ?   ?

See answer 93.

BRAIN TWISTERS — Puzzle 161

How much is the question mark worth?

1	6	6
7	8	56
9	7	?

See answer 40.

HEADSCRATCHERS — Puzzle 162

What letter does the question mark represent ?

44	Q L A	30
? O Y		H T U
33	I F R	49

See answer 100.

How much is the question mark worth?

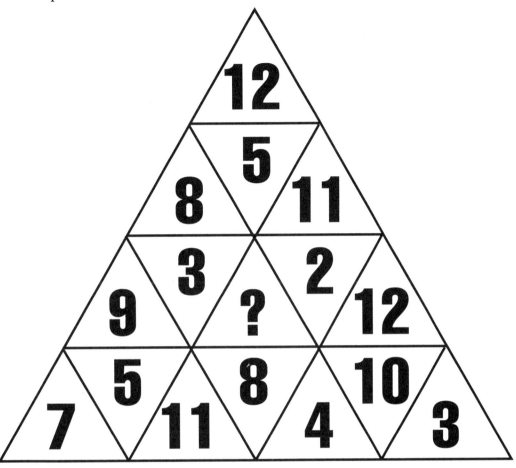

See answer 90.

How much is the question mark worth?

See answer 159.

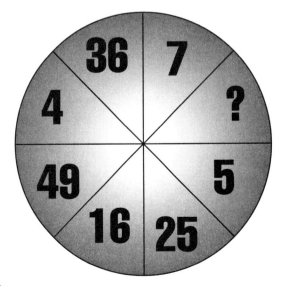

How much is the question mark worth?

See answer 152.

19	513	27
52	?	3
14	182	13

Insert one of the four basic mathematical signs in each space to complete the sum, starting from the top. One sign is used twice, the rest once. Each letter represents its position in the alphabet, where A = 1 and Z = 26.

+ − X ÷

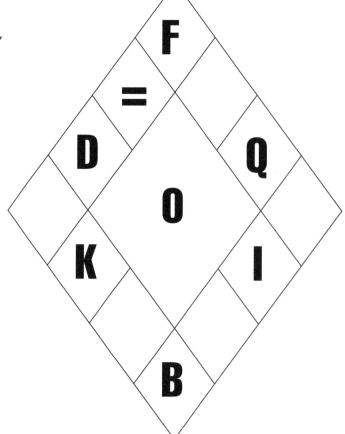

See answer 115.

How much is the question mark worth?

A	B	C	D	E
5	3	7	23	33
12	2	2	12	16
8	9	10	56	114
6	4	8	35	45
5	7	6	40	?

See answer 228.

Each pattern is worth either 1, 3, 5 or 7 points. The total value is 34. What is each pattern worth?

See answer 155.

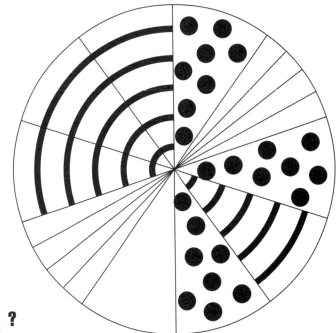

 ?   ?   ?   ?

ANSWERS

Answer 1
The Nile.

Answer 2
He isn't dead.

Answer 3
A clock with a second hand.

Answer 4
Wait until dusk when the frogs climb out of the water and go hunting.

Answer 5
He held it 2.5 metres (eight feet) above the floor. True, it fell two metres without breaking but, on hitting the floor, it smashed to smithereens!

Answer 6
The frog will never reach the edge.

Answer 7
Place the first egg in the middle. Every time your opponent places an egg you must place one diametrically opposite his. That way you will always place the final egg.

Answer 8
Charlie is in the garden laying turf for a lawn.

QUICK WIT Answer 9
He was a tourist looking for a souvenir and shot the sergeant with a camera.

Answer 10
All except February.

Answer 11
If hyperbolic acid could eat its way through anything, you could not put it in a flask.

QUICK WIT Answer 12
Captains don't lead battalions.

Answer 13
D.

Answer 14
4. Products of pairs of numbers facing each other equals 24.

Answer 15
The wife was heavily pregnant. While her husband was away she went into labour and had twins which, being a resourceful woman, she delivered herself.

Answer 16
He remembered too late why he had come in the first place – the electric window winder on the driver's door was broken and the window was open.

Answer 17
Polar Bears are only found in the Arctic (North Pole).

Answer 18
Candles for birthday cakes.

Answer 19
He stuck a small piece of sticky tape to the balloon and pushed the pin through the tape.

Answer 20
The date, like the islanders, does not exist.

Answer 21
E.

Answer 22
E. In all other cases the letters, if reflected along an imaginary vertical line, still form a letter.

Answer 23
No, they would be moonquakes.

Answer 24
Only once. After that you are subtracting from 44, 42, etc.

QUICK WIT Answer 25
No. He was confusing himself by thinking in terms of years (a purely arbitrary measure of time). What was happening was that the carbon dioxide level rose and then, some months later, so did the temperature.

QUICK WIT Answer 26
The third horse was a clothes horse.

Answer 27
The flat was in the spare.

SUPER SLEUTH Answer 28
The dead man was a mechanic. He had been servicing the car while the owner went on holiday. While he was working on the car the jack gave way and the car fell on him.

Answer 29
1. Starting with 64, subtract 1, 2, 4, 8, 16, 32, missing a number each time and working in a clockwise direction.

Answer 30
A door.

Answer 31
It was an adult movie and Dave's uncle is only ten years old.

Answer 32
8. Sequence of adding 2, subtracting 1, in the pattern followed by working round the triangle in the 2, 4, 3, 5, 4, 6, 5, 7, 6, 8, etc. pattern.

Answer 33
Dr Bicuspid. Since these are the only two dentists in town it is certain they do each other's dental work. Therefore Dr Molar must be responsible for the poor state of his partner's teeth and should be avoided.

QUICK WIT Answer 34
He had loaded the sacks with sand so they would actually get heavier after they had been in water.

Answer 35
Bartok, Delius, Mahler, Mozart, Puccini, Purcell Rachmaninov, Rimsky-Korsakov, Sibelius, Schubert.

Answer 36
As many times as you like. And the answer will always be 14.491297!

Answer 37
The wind is coming from the north but the road is going to the north.

Answer 38
2:1 on.

Answer 39
The truck was a car transporter and the cars were its cargo.

Answer 40
63. In each row, the product of the first 2 numbers equals the third.

Answer 41
B. Rotate the figure 90 degrees clockwise and reflect the curved lines.

Answer 42
C. In all other cases, the biggest shape is also the smallest.

Answer 43
18. Sum of the pairs of numbers facing each other equals 21.

Answer 44
E. The value of letter given by position in the alphabet is added together. An even answer should give a triangle, an odd answer a circle.

Answer 45
It is true that Sue and Hannah are sisters, but they are not each other's sisters.

Answer 46
So were the other half.

Answer 47
T (All the letters can be reversed laterally and remain the same).

Answer 48
C. The minute hand moves forward five minutes and the hour hand moves forward three hours.

Answer 49
Two (one on each side, each going in ever decreasing circles round to the hole in the middle).

Answer 130

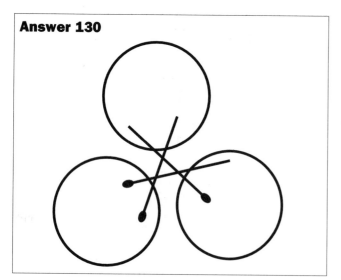

Answer 60

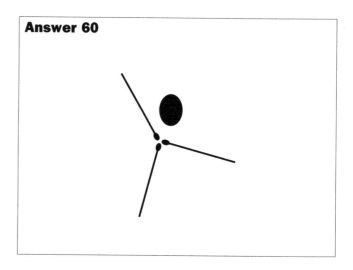

Answer 50
Frozen sea water contains much less salt than it does when liquid. By melting lumps of ice from the sea there would be ample water for the crew to drink.

Answer 51
Jim had retired as captain and was watching on TV. The papers compared the team's current miserable performance with it's fame under Jim's captaincy.

Answer 52
Two girls at the same time would mean buying three tickets. One girl twice would require four tickets as he buys for himself on both occasions.

Answer 53
'I've run away from home but I'm not old enough to cross the road myself!'

Answer 54
Neither – fish are cold-blooded.

Answer 55
You saw the explosion on TVs in a shop window.

Answer 56
A.

Answer 67

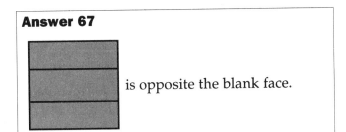 is opposite the blank face.

Answer 57

He got a bucket of water which he emptied into the hole to float the ball to the surface.

Answer 58

Black = 8; Speckled = 9.

Answer 59

C. When fish face outwards mouth should be open.

Answer 60

See diagram on Page 112.

Answer 61

D. All the others touch the sides in two separate places, but this one touches the sides in four places.

Answer 62

A whip.

Answer 63

Because 1884 is one more than 1883.

Answer 64

'Are you dead?'

Answer 65

No one. The barber was the mayor's wife.

Answer 66

The hours move back 3, 4, 5, and 6 hours. The minutes move forward 4, 8, 16, and 32 minutes. The seconds move back 1, 2, 3, and 4 seconds. The time on the fifth watch should be 21.14.51.

Answer 67

See box above.

Answer 68

4. The answer depends upon the number of the four-sided figures within which the number lies.

Answer 143

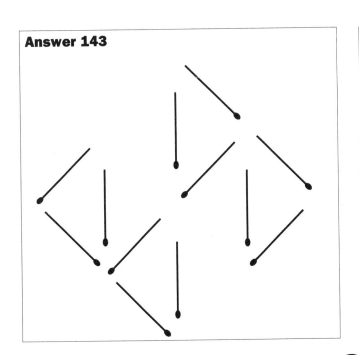

Answer 112

```
           86374
   19 1641106
      152
        121
        114
          71
          57
          140
          133
            76
```

Answer 133

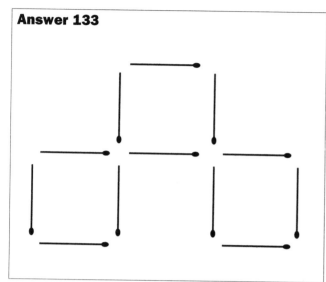

Answer 69

C. Curves are reflected. Horizontal and vertical lines interchange and diagonals go in opposite directions.

Answer 70

$3 \times 8 \div 6 + 7 \times 2 - 9 = 13$.

Answer 71

An armchair.

Answer 72

You would die. During the five seconds of your absence the earth would have travelled a considerable distance and you would be stranded in airless outer space.

Answer 73

120. Working clockwise starting from 9, each 2 adjacent small numbers are multiplied together to get the adjacent total.

Answer 74

Andy was a member of the ground crew. He climbed aboard the plane, serviced it and climbed right down again.

Answer 75

D. The vertical mirror image of w is m, the letter before n. The vertical mirror image of d is p, the letter before q.

Answer 76

It is spelt IT.

Answer 77

Fold the postcard and cut. See design on Page 117.

Answer 78

D. In all other cases the number of cross pieces on top of each vertical line is multiplied by the number of cross pieces on the bottom. All give even answers apart from D.

Answer 79

Penultimate triangle on the bottom row. Sequence, starting from the top and working from left to right, of dot, miss 1 triangle, dot, miss 2, dot, miss 3, dot, miss 4.

Answer 80

A die.

Answer 81

Albert was a lousy conductor!

Answer 82

There were five men present, but the dealer was a woman.

Answer 83

H (All the letters can be reversed vertically and remain the same).

Answer 84

The men are Siamese twins. The judge wants to know whether they can be separated.

Answer 136

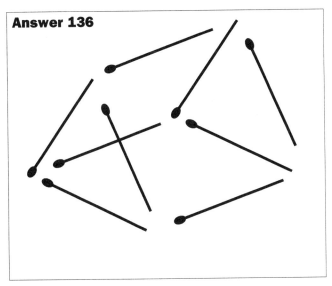

Answer 85
Time.

Answer 86
Over 16,000,000.

Answer 87
Mr White was, or at least his ashes. His last request was that his remains be interred in the local cemetery. The German authorities did not known who to address the urn to and came up with a rather strange solution to their dilemma.

Answer 88
O. The letters represent a number based on their position in the alphabet. The total for each triangle equals 60.

Answer 89
Inwards.

Answer 90
10. The numbers in each row of triangles equal 12, 24, 36, 48, when added together, starting from the top.

Answer 91
Fortunately they reach the bridge at different times.

Answer 92
The man was left-handed. He was injured on a Saturday and went back to work on Monday morning.

Answer 93
Radiating lines = 2; Curved lines = 4; Black = 6.

Answer 94
39. The sum of each adjacent pair of top numbers is halved to get the value underneath.

Answer 95
$5. The men were a grandfather, his son and grandson.

Answer 96
The arteries, veins and capillaries in your own body.

Answer 97
$14 \times 2 \div 7 + 11 - 4 \times 6 = 66$.

Answer 98
Dinosaurs and humans never lived at the same time so cave men were never eaten by dinosaurs.

Answer 129
Make a triangle flat on the table and hold the other matches over it to make a pyramid.

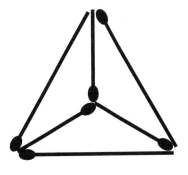

Answer 99

B. The figure moves 90 degrees clockwise each time. When diamond is either north or south, then the circle and square change to shaded and unshaded respectively and the arrowhead becomes a square with a diagonal line.

Answer 100

D. Letters take their value from their order in the alphabet, where A = 1, Z = 26. Each 3 letters are added together to give the value at the end of each set, so Q + L + A = 30, moving in a clockwise direction.

Answer 101

61 times.

Answer 102

There are more of them.

Answer 103

If he takes three socks from the drawer he must have a pair, however, since it is totally dark he will still not know which ones he put on!

Answer 138

Pick up the matchbox by forefinger and thumb and bring the case up to your mouth. Suck gently to make the tray stick to the case and then very carefully turn the whole thing over.

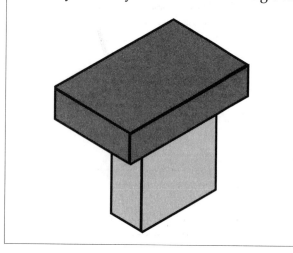

Answer 146

The sum also works as V11-11=V

Answer 104

A. It is the number of spaces beween the crosses.

3	**X**	1
2	3	4
X	1	2

3	**X**	1
2	**X**	1
X	1	2

X	1	2
3	**X**	1
2	3	4

X	1	2
3	**X**	1
2	**X**	1

X	1	2
X	1	2
3	**X**	1

Answer 105

Flowers = 5; Bubbles = 3; Birds Feet = 1.

Answer 106

K. Position order of the first letter minus that of the second in each section gives the answer next to it e.g. T – N = 6, moving in a clockwise direction.

Answer 107

No, sharks don't sleep.

Answer 108

An hourglass.

Answer 109

B.

Answer 110

5+ ins to the middle.

Answer 111

A square. If the three numbers around the triangle add to an even number the shape is a square; if it is odd, then it is another triangle.

Answer 141

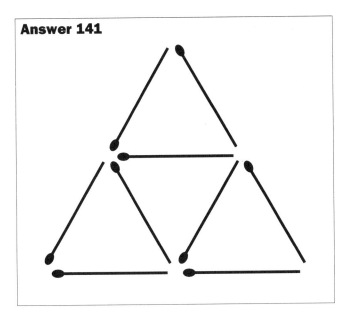

Answer 112
See working on Page 113.

Answer 113
Vertical lines = 2; Blank = 4; Horizontal lines = 6; Zig-zag = 8.

Answer 114
R. Number preceding each pair of letters shows how many letters the second letter is after the first, e.g. P is 5 letters after K in alphabetical order.

Answer 115
F + Q x I + B ÷ K – D = O.

QUICK WIT Answer 116
Zulfiqa Khan was smuggling donkeys.

Answer 117
The mirror actually reverses you back to front.

Answer 118
Because they are two of a set of triplets.

Answer 119
D. Add a cross piece each time, alternating between adding them vertically and horizontally. A vertical cross piece changes the colour of the arrow head.

Answer 120
A.

Answer 121
L – G x F ÷ C + O ÷ E = E.

Answer 122
N. The numbers in each block are added together, then count back from the end of the alphabet that many times to find the letter next to each block (7 2 5 is linked to M and so on). The letter follows the numbers in a clockwise direction.

Answer 123
Press hard on one coin and then use a third coin to strike it smartly on the edge. The force will be transmitted to the coin you mustn't touch which will then skid across the table allowing ample room for the book.

Answer 77

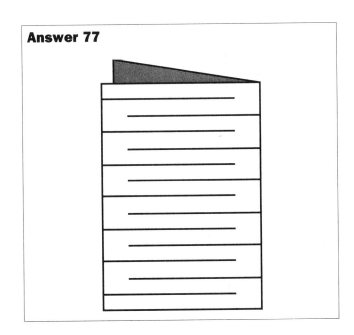

Answer 142

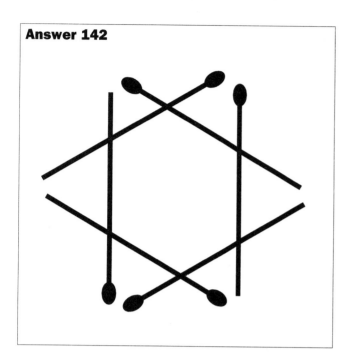

Answer 124

$27 \div 9 \times 6 + 12 \div 3 - 5 = 5$.

Answer 125

The air above the Equator is much colder than the air over the Poles (because at the point there is a greater height of air and therefore the temperature can fall lower).

Answer 126

Although deaf he was not mute, so he shouted 'Shark!'

Answer 127

Fish.

Answer 128

The conductor's baton.

Answer 129

See design on Page 115.

Answer 130

See design on Page 112.

Answer 131

14

Answer 132

53. The 2 top numbers in each column are added together to give the value underneath.

Answer 133

See design on Page 114.

Answer 134

See design on Page 121.

Answer 135

See design on Page 122.

Answer 136

See design on Page 115.

Answer 137

Push the tray of each box slightly forward and then fit the boxes into each other. This should make quite a strong tower which can be picked up without collapsing.

Answer 138

See design on Page 116.

Answer 145

IV + I = V

Answer 139
Put your face directly above the coins and blow very hard into the glass. With a little practice you should be able to get the small coin to jump out onto the table.

Answer 140
See design on Page 124.

Answer 141
See design on Page 117

Answer 142
See design on Page 118.

Answer 143
See design on Page 113.

Answer 144
See design above right.

Answer 145
See design on Page 118.

Answer 146
See design on Page 116.

Answer 147
See design on Page 121.

Answer 148
Move yourself! If viewed upside down the equation is correct.

Answer 149
See design on right.

Answer 150
See design on Page 120.

Answer 144

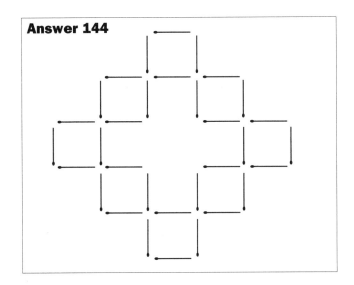

Answer 151

x	+	-
x	x	÷
÷	x	+
x	+	-
÷	x	x

Answer 152
156. In each row, the first number multiplied by the third equals the second.

Answer 149

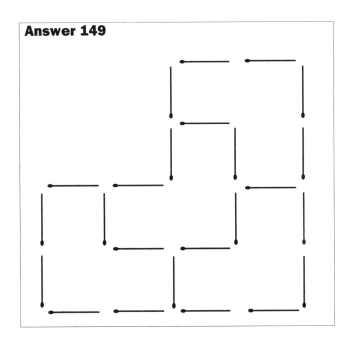

Answer 153
B. The minute hand moves back fifteen minutes and the hour hand moves forward three hours.

Answer 154
D. The second hand moves forward 30 and back 15 seconds alternately, the minute hand moves back 10 and forward five minutes alternately, and the hour hand moves forward two and back one hour alternately.

Answer 155
Dots = 1; Curved lines = 3; Blank = 5; Straight lines = 7.

Answer 156
F is wrong. In all the others the dot is in both the square and the triangle.

Answer 157
Ben Gurion, Gatwick, Las Palmas.

Answer 158
Heathrow, McCoy, O'Hare, Dalaman, Dar Es Salaam, Ho Chi Minh City, Houston, El Paso, Charles De Gaulle, Benito Juarez, Kranebitten.

Answer 159
6. Every small number also has its square value in the circle.

Answer 160
A La Recherche Du Temps Perdu, A Thousand And One Nights, To Kill A Mockingbird.

Answer 161
Edward Albee, Samuel Beckett, Bertholt Brecht, Noel Coward, Anton Chekov, Arthur Miller, Luigi Pirandello, Jean Racine, Sophocles, Tennessee Williams.

Answer 162
Sibling. All the others refer to a specific sex.

Answer 163
Your ship is a space ship and the sea is one of the seas of the moon.

Answer 164
He folded his arms, picked up the ends of the string, unfolded the arms and, hey presto, a knot!

Answer 165
See design on Page 127.

Answer 166
See design on Page 128.

Answer 167
See design on Page 126.

Answer 168
Jodie Foster, Marlon Brando, Cybill Shepherd, Claudia Cardinale, Roman Polanski, Daniel Day Lewis, Robert Redford, Walter Matthau, Woody Allen, Dudley Moore.

Answer 169
Because a round cover cannot fall back down a hole.

Answer 150

Answer 147

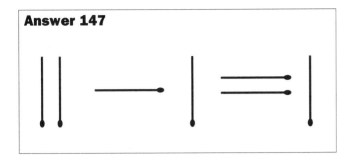

Answer 170

Augustus, Caligula, Claudius, Diocletian, Galba, Nero, Tiberius, Trajan, Valerian, Vespasian.

Answer 179

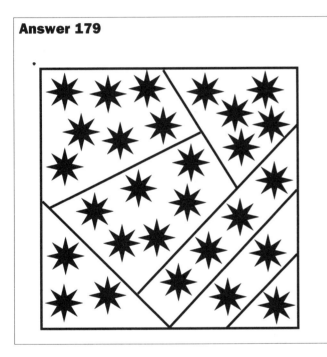

Answer 171

Bobby Ford in the Bronx isn't married to Donna, Anna, Betsy, or Joan, so he must be married to Mary whose former husband was Dick Jones. Mary didn't come from the Bronx, Queens, Staten Island or Manhattan, so she must have come from Brooklyn. Bobby didn't come from the Bronx or Brooklyn, Queens or Manhattan, so he must have come from Staten Island, which means his former wife was Betsy. Joan Martin's former husband was wasn't Bobby or Dick, Hank or Dave (her present husband), so he must be Jim Lewis from Manhattan. She and Dave can't live in the Bronx or Manhattan, Brooklyn or Staten Island, so they must live in Queens. Dave didn't come from Brooklyn, Staten Island, Manhattan or Queens, so he must have come from the Bronx. His former wife wasn't Mary, Anna or Betsy, so she must have been Donna. Dick Jones married to Betsy, came from Brooklyn. He doesn't live in the Bronx, Brooklyn, Queens or Staten Island, so he must live in Manhattan. Jim Lewis from Manhattan Joan's former husband), is married to Anna Smith from Queens and lives in Brooklyn. Therefore Hank Smith married Donna from the Bronx and they live in Staten Island.

	Ex-Wife	Ex-Home	New Wife	New Home
Bobby Ford	Betsy	Staten I.	Mary	Bronx
Dick Jones	Mary	Brooklyn	Betsy	M'hattar
Jim Lewis	Joan	M'hattan	Anna	Brooklyn
Dave Martin	Donna	Bronx	Joan	Queens
Hank Smith	Anna	Queens	Donna	Staten I.

Answer 172

1st: John (68 min, 22 sec)
2nd: Ivan (68 min, 27 sec)
3rd: Bruce (68 min, 35 sec)
4th: Pedro (68 min, 40 sec)
5th: Pierre (68 min, 53 sec).

Answer 134

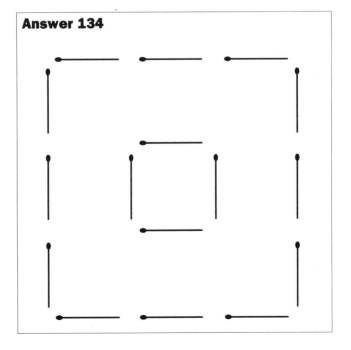

Answer 135
The square root of 1 is 1.

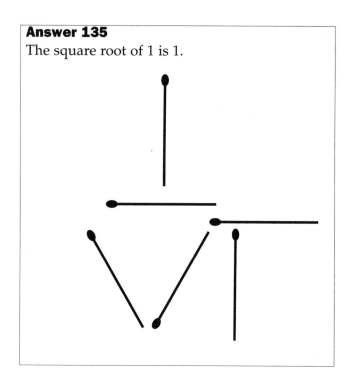

Answer 176
Piece A. The pattern is 2 circles, 2 squares, 2 triangles; 3 circles, 2 squares, 3 triangles; 1 circle, 2 squares, 1 triangle repeated. The pattern starts at the top right and goes round the grid clockwise in an inward spiral.

Answer 177
As Neville has a drive five times longer than that of Pauline, and they drive for 60 minutes between them, Neville must have a 50-minute journey in the sports car and Pauline a 10-minute drive. Lynda's drive is five times the length of Martin's so she must have a 25-minute journey, while Martin has a 5-minute drive in his estate car, because it is half of Pauline's journey time. Therefore, Olivia has a 40-minute drive in the saloon, Pauline is in the van and Lynda drives the convertible.

Lynda	25 minutes	convertible
Martin	5 minutes	estate
Neville	50 minutes	sports
Olivia	40 minutes	saloon
Pauline	10 minutes	van

Answer 173

72	÷	9	x	5	=	40
−		−		+		÷
18	+	6	−	4	=	20
54	÷	3	÷	9	=	2

Answer 174
Piece C. The pattern is 3 hearts, 3 diamonds, 3 spades; 2 hearts, 2 diamonds, 2 spades; 1 heart, 1 diamond and 1 spade repeated. It starts at the top left corner and moves back and forth across the grid in a boustrophedon pattern.

Answer 175
Piece B. The sequence is 3 stars, 2 triangles, 1 cross; 1 star, 2 triangles, 3 crosses; 3 stars, 3 triangles, 3 crosses repeated. The pattern starts at the bottom left and repeats in a vertical boustrophedon.

Answer 178

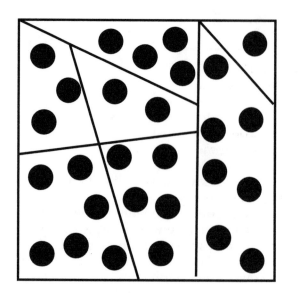

Answer 178
See design on Page 122.

Answer 179
See design on Page 121.

Answer 180
Dustin Hoffman   Derek Jacobi
Paul Newman   Julia Roberts
Arnold Schwarzenegger
Anjelica Huston   Demi Moore
Nastassja Kinski   Winona Ryder

Answer 181
B. There is no triangle intersection on the odd one.

Answer 182
D. The shape is laterally transposed and then reflected down the dividing line.

Answer 183
C.

Answer 184
B. The sequence here is less one dot, plus two dots, and the box rotates in a clockwise direction for each dot.

Answer 185
D. All except D have odd number of edges.

Answer 186
We are talking about a chess game.

Answer 187
D. Circle and triangle alternate. After a circle the next figure moves round one space, staying on the same side of the line. After a triangle it moves on 2.

Answer 188
E. Left half reflected to form symmetrical shape, then half of right half is reflected back.

Answer 189
A.

Answer 190
C. The smallest segment is rotated 90 degrees clockwise. The middle segment remains static. Largest segment rotated 90 degrees anti or counter clockwise.

Answer 191
B.

Answer 192
E. Largest shape is reflected horizontally and the size order is reversed.

Answer 193
B. In all other cases the smaller circle is within the larger circle.

Answer 194
E. A dotted V shape is added each time with dots alternating between being at the start and at the end of each V added. The leading edge of a new V overlaps the undotted edge of the previous V.

Answer 195
Andy's mother and aunt were identical twins.

Answer 196
D. An unshaded ringed planet becomes a shaded ringed planet; a star containing a shaded planet becomes an unshaded planet; a shaded ringed planet becomes an unshaded ringed planet; an unshaded planet becomes a star containing a shaded planet. The symbols are then vertically reflected.

Answer 197
They are sisters.

Answer 198
You don't bury survivors.

Answer 199
Only one – after that it isn't empty any more.

Answer 200
B.

Answer 201
E. Rotate one place clockwise and then reflect across a horizontal line through the middle of the figure.

Answer 202
D. Top row of letters go back in alphabetical order 3 places each time. The middle row goes forward 2, 3, 4, 5 places. Bottom row goes back 8, 4, 2, 1 places.

Answer 203
Yes. And a 5th, 6th, 7th...

Answer 204
9. Each vowel is worth 4. Each consonant is worth 3. The sum of each set of letters gives the total following each set, in a clockwise direction.

Answer 205
A. A single line can be added to make three, not upside down, capital letters. The others already have 3.

Answer 206
He decided to go for a binge on the way home, got talking, and didn't arrive home until 6.43 the following morning.

Answer 207
C. Curved lines gradually encroach on space within triangle.

Answer 208
D. One tip of the star is missing.

Answer 209
D. Add 2 lines, then 1, 2, 1. Rotate slightly each time.

Answer 210
C. Small square becomes a big square and vice versa. A small square with a triangle goes to small square alone. A triangle on big square remains a triangle.

Answer 140

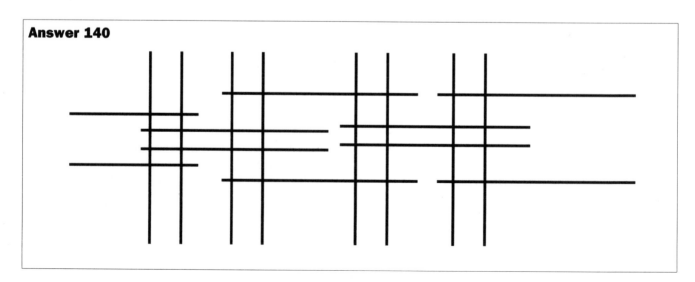

Answer 211
Only 30 minutes. The alarm clock went off at 9.00 pm.

Answer 212
D. One end of the rectangle should fit inside the circle. The arrow should cut through the rectangle in such a way as to make 2 four sided shapes. The arrow must be outside the circle.

Answer 213
A. In the other cases the addition of a vertical or horizontal straight line would form a capital letter.

Answer 214
He was talking about his heart.

Answer 215
A. The inner shape becomes outer shape,the shape surrounding it fits inside, then shape at top. The remainder is then shrunk and put inside the middle shape. A shaded shape covers an unshaded shape.

Answer 216
C. It is the only instance where a square is not touching a triangle.

Answer 217
D. The diagonal line sloping up from left to right becomes horizontal. Vertical lines stay vertical. Diagonal lines sloping down from left to right slope up. Where a square contains a triangle the whole square is flipped vertically.

Answer 218
They were buying digits for their house number. Four at $3 each cost $12.

Answer 219
A circle in the second triangle on the bottom row. Starting from the top, working from left to right, sequence of square, miss 2 , triangle, circle, miss 1, square, miss 2, and so on.

Answer 220
False teeth.

Answer 221
He shaves.

Answer 222
C, the rectangle. A shape with an odd number of edges is followed by one with an even number, working down from left to right.

Answer 223
C.

Answer 224
D. If you add together the total number of sides of all the shapes, D is the only one with an odd total.

Answer 225
A. The middle shape becomes the outside shape. A shaded shape covers an unshaded shape.

Answer 226
B. In all other cases there are two white and two black triangles at the corners.

Answer 227
B. The number of straight lines doubles each time

Answer 228
32. Working along each row from left to right, (A + B) x C – D = E.

Answer 229
F. The number 8 is the only one which is symmetrical.

Answer 167

G	A	C	H	I	N	A	T	O	W	N	U	L	H	V	R	E	G	S	O
Z	R	B	L	T	N	O	S	I	D	A	M	I	Y	X	N	N	O	I	P
R	T	E	U	A	C	S	B	L	D	F	G	T	H	R	T	R	K	M	E
A	L	G	E	P	R	Q	Q	S	A	C	T	T	A	V	Z	Y	X	A	H
R	I	B	Q	N	Z	N	O	U	P	R	C	L	A	C	B	A	L	A	A
S	N	K	A	C	W	R	A	M	A	B	R	E	I	T	A	L	Y	I	L
D	C	G	E	L	E	I	O	N	D	R	O	N	N	O	T	T	I	L	N
G	O	H	A	T	M	N	C	E	W	C	E	T	A	H	S	T	L	U	E
S	L	W	N	A	V	E	S	H	E	Y	G	I	T	H	A	I	S	N	I
S	N	E	A	P	A	I	V	M	N	A	I	M	N	T	H	R	E	H	A
R	C	S	E	G	E	I	I	T	R	T	I	E	S	G	M	O	L	Q	N
C	I	T	Y	E	L	E	Y	O	D	E	N	S	Q	U	A	R	E	E	U
L	L	A	H	L	H	T	O	F	L	A	Y	T	A	D	I	U	M	R	M
L	T	O	A	N	B	R	O	N	X	C	S	P	A	R	K	N	I	S	L
I	K	G	E	E	G	E	T	T	R	I	E	E	K	N	A	Y	N	G	B
L	E	S	O	G	O	D	F	E	R	O	M	L	A	S	T	R	O	O	N
E	I	T	O	G	A	T	M	E	W	R	F	I	A	T	I	I	N	N	G
T	H	H	E	U	S	A	E	B	L	O	I	N	G	T	P	U	Z	B	Z
L	O	E	S	G	R	A	L	D	T	H	E	G	N	I	D	L	I	U	T
T	I	M	E	G	I	T	B	R	O	O	K	L	Y	N	I	S	A	P	A

Answer 165

```
M I F T E P Z L E I R U E P D T M E R B
A A D I H U Z N E S H A L E R O H N E O
N G D H T E I E M S A A E R M S U E M I
C H H E S E Y O E S F G S E U T B L U S
A R D E L L I W N A F A O L E I I L T D
G A R D E O N D E I Y Y N A W N L L R E
Y T R E O A M T H M R E I C L H R A S B
O D E C H D E P E O W T L H T E Y O S O
U T H C T Y A R S P S T E A F R A N U U
M E A T H E C O M E O E D I O D E G O L
M J A R D I N D O U L E G S S A C R E O
C H C T P R E E R N H Y R E R U E O C G
A R A E R S A S A D T I S D J U I K H N
T C A R S A D P F N I S E I S T L E T E
C T O H C I S L E L I B E R T E L I L E
L E P R E D D A N T E S S E A Y L T T S
I Y E S T E G M T M O N T M A R T R E O
C T R E T Y R U E D E R I V O L I D O N
H H A R W A T H E Y A B E E N E T U O R
Y N D I O M P H E H V E L O U V R E E A
```

Answer 166

A	N	O	W	T	H	W	E	S	T	M	I	N	S	T	E	R	E	K	R
B	C	L	A	Q	P	O	D	Y	U	P	D	P	Z	Z	L	E	F	I	I
N	I	H	T	S	I	H	E	S	T	I	Y	U	U	A	R	E	D	N	W
H	A	E	E	C	N	A	R	E	T	L	H	C	E	Q	S	E	P	G	E
O	P	R	R	L	C	E	G	O	L	I	N	G	I	T	S	O	C	S	O
U	I	G	L	O	O	A	H	I	U	W	P	S	R	O	M	R	E	C	C
A	S	N	H	T	H	A	D	T	S	H	W	H	C	U	S	A	A	R	T
I	G	C	W	A	S	O	H	O	N	I	T	T	O	K	O	H	G	O	E
R	E	I	R	S	I	M	L	J	G	T	I	N	G	N	W	L	M	S	Y
G	U	T	O	O	T	N	E	D	G	E	H	A	L	L	A	U	N	S	T
A	N	S	D	W	S	S	H	R	T	A	T	D	O	F	B	O	G	K	I
G	O	L	D	E	N	E	T	A	O	F	O	R	A	M	D	Y	N	T	R
O	L	E	B	S	O	U	K	G	W	E	Y	R	U	N	C	K	A	I	L
U	B	A	Q	S	L	R	T	T	E	L	T	F	O	A	P	L	G	H	T
E	I	U	F	Y	A	O	N	U	R	O	F	L	L	A	M	C	A	N	S
R	A	R	O	P	A	E	E	T	H	S	T	A	Y	A	U	E	A	B	Y
E	A	D	E	L	V	R	L	G	I	N	C	S	H	O	R	L	R	L	A
R	A	D	M	O	R	A	L	E	E	E	C	G	P	A	R	I	E	T	Y
E	Y	S	C	A	T	B	U	C	K	I	N	W	H	A	D	Y	N	O	U
H	N	O	T	C	H	E	L	S	E	A	J	O	E	G	R	K	Z	O	O